A BEWITCHING PLACE

Samuel Clemens—Mark Twain—and his family gathered for a photograph on the porch of their house in 1885. From the left are his daughter Clara; his wife, Livy; his daughter Jean; Samuel himself; and his daughter Susy. The dog is Hash, one of many Clemens pets. THE MARK TWAIN HOUSE & MUSEUM. GIFT OF THE HARPERS.

A BEWITCHING PLACE

THE STORY OF THE **MARK TWAIN HOUSE** IN HARTFORD

STEVE COURTNEY

Photographs by John Groo
Foreword by Hal Holbrook
Introduction by David Baldacci

Essex, Connecticut

Dedicated to Walter K. Schwinn (1901–1995), the historian of Mark Twain's house, and to Michael J. Kiskis (1954–2011), Twain scholar and friend.

The publication of this edition of *The Bewitching House* was made possible with support from Stanley Black & Decker.

Globe Pequot

An imprint of The Globe Pequot Publishing Group, Inc.
64 S Main St.
Essex, CT 06426
www.GlobePequot.com

Distributed by NATIONAL BOOK NETWORK

Copyright © 2025 by The Mark Twain House & Museum
First edition published 2011 by Dover Publishing as *"The Loveliest Home That Ever Was"*

Photos © 2025 by The Mark Twain House & Museum

All rights reserved. No part of this book may be reproduced in any form or by any electronic or mechanical means, including information storage and retrieval systems, without written permission from the publisher, except by a reviewer who may quote passages in a review.

British Library Cataloguing in Publication Information available

Library of Congress Cataloging-in-Publication Data
Names: Courtney, Steve, 1948– author. | Groo, John, photographer. | Holbrook, Hal, writer of foreword. | Baldacci, David, writer of introduction.
Title: A bewitching place : the story of the Mark Twain House in Hartford / Steve Courtney ; photographs by John Groo ; foreword by Hal Holbrook ; introduction by David Baldacci.
Description: Essex, Connecticut : Globe Pequot, 2025. | Includes bibliographical references. | Summary: "This book is the official guide to the Mark Twain House & Museum, an institution dedicated to preserving the author's home, literary legacy, and life story. Steve Courtney conducts a journey back to the Gilded Age, when the celebrated author and humorist was known as Mr. Samuel Clemens of Hartford, Connecticut. Readers can venture inside this 'bewitching' landmark for an illustrated tour that offers intimate glimpses of the writer, his wife, and their daughters within their Victorian mansion"— Provided by publisher.
Identifiers: LCCN 2024059399 (print) | LCCN 2024059400 (ebook) | ISBN 9781493091102 (cloth) | ISBN 9781493091119 (epub)
Subjects: LCSH: Mark Twain House (Hartford, Conn.) | Twain, Mark, 1835–1910—Homes and haunts—Connecticut—Hartford.
Classification: LCC PS1334 .C677 2025 (print) | LCC PS1334 (ebook) | DDC 818/.409–dc23/eng/20241220
LC record available at https://lccn.loc.gov/2024059399
LC ebook record available at https://lccn.loc.gov/2024059400

Printed in India

The house & grounds are not to be described, they are so beautiful. . . . I don't think I ever saw such a bewitching place as ours is.
—SAMUEL LANGHORNE CLEMENS TO ORION CLEMENS, SEPTEMBER 21, 1874

How ugly, tasteless, repulsive, are all the domestic interiors I have ever seen in Europe compared with the perfect taste of this ground floor, with its delicious dream of harmonious color, & its all-pervading spirit of peace & serenity & deep contentment. You did it all, & it speaks of you & praises you eloquently & unceasingly. It is the loveliest home that ever was.
—SAMUEL LANGHORNE CLEMENS TO OLIVIA LANGDON CLEMENS, MARCH 20, 1895

To us, our house was not unsentient matter—it had a heart, & a soul, & eyes to see us with; & approvals, & solicitudes, & deep sympathies; it was of us, & we were in its confidence, & lived in its grace & in the peace of its benediction. We never came home from an absence that its face did not light up & speak out its eloquent welcome—& we could not enter it unmoved.
—SAMUEL LANGHORNE CLEMENS TO JOSEPH HOPKINS TWICHELL, JANUARY 19, 1897

Many of the readers of The Times, doubtless, have had at least an external view of the structure, which already has acquired something beyond a local fame; and such persons, we think, will agree with us in the opinion that it is one of the oddest looking buildings in the State ever designed for a dwelling, if not the whole country.
—*HARTFORD DAILY TIMES*, MARCH 23, 1874

Contents

FOREWORD TO THE 2011 EDITION *HAL HOLBROOK* IX
INTRODUCTION *DAVID BALDACCI* XI
PREFACE: A TOUR WITH MARY MASON FAIRBANKS XIII

CHAPTER ONE
"Am Pretty Well Known, Now—
Intend to Be Better Known"
1

CHAPTER TWO
"That Birth-Place of Six-Shooters"
10

CHAPTER THREE
"They Preferred Mr. Potter to Everyone Else"
15

CHAPTER FOUR
A Tour of the House
27

CHAPTER FIVE
"The House Is Still Full of Carpenters"
110

CHAPTER SIX
"O Never Revamp a House!"
123

CHAPTER SEVEN
"I Wish There Was Some Way to
Change Our Manner of Living"
129

CHAPTER EIGHT
"I Knew Mark Twain"
140

BACKSTAGE AT A BEWITCHING PLACE 153
BIBLIOGRAPHY 164
ABOUT THE AUTHOR 168

Foreword to the 2011 Edition

WHAT CAN I SAY ABOUT THE MARK TWAIN HOUSE except that I love it and its atmosphere. I have been fortunate to see its reconstruction from near the beginning and to watch its gracious charm and dignity come back in polished butternut and gold design. I see in memory those extraordinary Hartford people who made this happen: Edie Salsbury, Atwood Collins, Bob Schutz, and many others who saved this house from demolition, rolled up their sleeves, restored it to its early grandeur, and made a miracle happen.

We can only recapture the past for a future generation by preserving it, allowing them to measure their own way of life against its presence and to find what is precious in it. In Mark Twain's Hartford house, its design inspired in places by his own mischievous vision, the memories of its former great tenant and his family seem to whisper there in the rooms and on the porches—a way of life gone long ago and dearer now for the loss of it.

—Hal Holbrook
Los Angeles, California

Introduction

LIVING WITH HIS WIFE AND THEIR THREE DAUGHTERS in the Hartford house represented the most idyllic phase in the long life of Samuel Clemens, also known as Mark Twain. His children were young, healthy, and suitably adoring of their famous father. His wife, Olivia ("Livy"), who endearingly called him "Youth," was the mistress of this fine mansion, one of the most eccentric buildings ever to be erected on American soil. She was also probably close to the healthiest she would ever be, and safe from harm, which was critical, for Clemens loved her above all others.

The Hartford home represented many important things to Clemens: financial success (although it was Livy's family money that fueled its construction); his arrival in Connecticut high society; a stable place to lay his head at night (for an itinerant nomad who was sometimes homeless, that was no small thing); and the opportunity to be, for the first time in his life, master of his own domain.

I have always been drawn to one particular photo of the Clemens family on the *ombra* (Italian for "shade"), a roofed porch that runs along the front of the Hartford house. Clemens is lean and youthful, dressed in a sharp three-piece suit, and is glancing off nobly to his left. Susy, his oldest daughter and favorite child, is seated, her head gracefully turned as she gives the lens a look that is part curiosity and part amusement. Livy is looking at the baby, Jean, who stares out with wide eyes, while a hatted Clara leans possessively into her father, with a petulant expression captured forevermore.

The scene is one of peace and serenity, family, love, a hint of mischievousness, a touch of sibling jealousy, and, above all, closeness. The backdrop to all this is a vine-covered post that holds up the *ombra*'s roof.

And that is what the Hartford home did for them: it *shaded* them, protected them, allowed them to be free of what was to come—the financial ruin, personal loss, and the grief that always accompanies it, and, finally, the end of all that had made Samuel Clemens perhaps the happiest person on earth. Indeed, what his home meant to him coincidentally reflected the literal meaning of his famous pseudonym, since Mark Twain, in steamboat piloting parlance, translates as *safe water*.

Clemens labored on the third floor of his home to create many of his finest works. He played billiards, often alone, late into the night, as his family slept peacefully beneath him. He may well have believed that this perfect life would never end, his wife and children, and himself, all frozen in their most satisfied state, and he, the biggest beneficiary of this seeming stoppage in the passage of time.

He may at times have taken for granted this sweet spot of his life, perhaps never anticipating or, more likely, never wanting to think about change ever happening. After all, writers are notoriously nostalgic; we remember so much from our pasts, which are reliable fuel and fodder for our creative sparks, because those memories often inspire the passion that the fashioning of tall tales requires.

Yet, after losing his favorite daughter in the very place that was supposed to be his family's safe haven, and subsequently never returning to the house again to live, Clemens nonetheless continued to dote on his old home. To him, the abode was not simply sticks and bricks but the sum total of his spirit, his creative soul, and the gathering place of his cherished family, where all was right, if not with *the* world, at least with *his* world.

Safely ensconced in a bewitching place.

—David Baldacci
Fairfax County, Virginia

Preface
A TOUR WITH MARY MASON FAIRBANKS

"THE HOUSE STANDS UPON FARMINGTON AVENUE," Mary Mason Fairbanks wrote in 1874 when Mark Twain's home in Hartford, Connecticut, was still under construction, "and is an attractive combination of dark red brick, set off by light graceful woodwork about the windows and balconies. It is planted as it were upon the bank of a dell at just the right angle to take in through its broad windows the loveliest of views of river, meadow, glen, and woodland." Fairbanks was no ordinary visitor to the Mark Twain House, but rather a close friend, mentor, and maternal spirit to Samuel L. Clemens. The author was just thirty-eight years old that year, though already famous for a tale of a jumping frog and other short sketches; for wildly humorous and lyrical book-length narratives of travel in Europe, the Holy Land, the American West, and Hawaii; and for a sprawling collaborative novel of Washington politics.

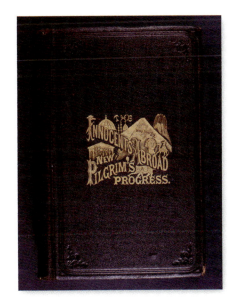

The cover of the first edition of *The Innocents Abroad* reflects the Victorian fascination with exoticism and American fascination with culture, with its images of the Great Pyramid of Giza, the Sphinx, and the Parthenon. The travel book remained Samuel Clemens's bestseller throughout his lifetime. THE MARK TWAIN HOUSE & MUSEUM COLLECTIONS.

Fairbanks, only seven years older, had met Clemens on the five-month voyage on the steamer *Quaker City* that had led to his bestseller—it was to remain his bestseller all through his life—*The Innocents Abroad: Or, the New Pilgrim's Progress*. She had been the center of Clemens's shipboard coterie; he nicknamed her "Mother" in a way that betokened relationship, not age. She lived in Ohio, where her husband owned the *Cleveland Herald*, but distance didn't prevent her from playing a key role as confidante in Clemens's courtship of Olivia Langdon of Elmira, New York, and from reassuring the heiress's parents about the basic goodness of her strange suitor.

The architect Edward Tuckerman Potter took Samuel Clemens's friend, Mary Mason Fairbanks, on a tour through the house while it was under construction in the spring of 1874. Potter was best known as a church architect in the Gothic style, an "ecclesiologist." THE MARK TWAIN HOUSE & MUSEUM COLLECTIONS.

Now married to Olivia Langdon Clemens—"Livy"—for four years, Clemens had been in a rush to get off to Elmira on a family visit when Fairbanks and her son Charles showed up in Hartford in April. Perhaps for that reason, it was Edward Tuckerman Potter, the architect, who took her on a tour of the house that he was building while the Clemenses leased a home nearby.

Fairbanks paused the reader on the threshold, in a piece she wrote for the *Herald*:

> Once more I am reminded that I cannot "draw a house," but I can give you the benefit of my tour of inspection through its numerous rooms, under the escort of the architect, Mr. Edward L. [sic] Potter, of New York. I hardly know which most impressed me, Mr. Potter's power in his art or his love of it. He gave me no detail of height or breadth, but in the quick effects which he helped me to discover I recognized the artist capable even of enthusing me, novice as I was, with a new interest in the wonderful science of architecture.

Here, at the broad, heavy entry door to Mark Twain's house, we leave her for the moment. If we can weave our own experience into the story, she is about to experience a sharp intake of breath—the same breath visitors take today as they enter the dimly lit, decorated entry hall of a man famous for his stories of life in the simple frame homes of a Missouri town, now transplanted to Gilded Age New England.

Curious visitors had started arriving around the same time Fairbanks did. A few months after her visit, Samuel himself, seated on the balcony outside his third-floor billiard room, turned from contemplating a muskrat swimming in the stream below to note, "The customary Sunday assemblage of strangers is gathered together in the grounds discussing the house." The customary assemblage is still there, Sunday and every other day.

At The Mark Twain House & Museum, we are devoted not only to preserving the author's home, literary legacy, and life story but also to satisfying our visitors' endless curiosity. This can extend from the mild interest of a tourist taking in the sights between the Statue of Liberty and the Foxwoods Resort Casino to the rapid-fire questions of a sixth-grade class, to the interest of the true Twainiac, armed with inquiries as to detail and fact. So when we were provided the opportunity to tell the house's story in new way, satisfying this curiosity and the great American love for Mark Twain in a book with photographs and commentary, we jumped at the chance.

Here are stories: the long wayward routes that brought a man from a small river port on the Mississippi to this leafy New England suburb; that brought a woman raised in wealth in a prosperous upstate New York canal port here; and what happened to them when they got to this place. It's a story of financial rise and fall, of literary labors that are hard to believe in their sheer quantity and the eloquent fire they spark, of a deeply loving family that fell from idyll to tragedy, and then to a kind of autumn revival, when Hartford was left behind. It's the story of the people who worked to keep the family's comfortable life going, laboring long hours to do so. It's the story of an architect charmed by the models he found in Europe and whose designs for churches, university halls, and floridly designed homes were tinged with a social conscience that took him to the tenements of New York City. There's the famed Louis C. Tiffany and another gifted interior designer, Candace Wheeler, a pioneer in her male-dominated age.

And there's the whole great, sprawling, vital, corrupt time in American history that Clemens dubbed "the Gilded Age," which has also been called an "Age of Energy." There's the city of Hartford, a bustling embodiment of that energy, with avenues of great wealth and labyrinths of deep poverty. There's the tale of what happened to the house in the years since the Clemenses sold it to a family whose small boy kept his pet alligator in the great glass conservatory, through its near-destruction in the 1920s, up to today, when it stands as the centerpiece of a famed house restoration–museum complex.

And at the center of it all, it's a story of the visitor—you—whom we take, with occasional commentary from Mary Mason Fairbanks, through the Mark Twain House room by room. Prepare for the intake of breath.

CHAPTER ONE

"Am Pretty Well Known, Now—Intend to Be Better Known"

After all these years I can picture that old time to myself now, just as it was then: the white town drowsing in the sunshine of a summer's morning; the streets empty, or pretty nearly so; one or two clerks in front of the Water Street stores, with their splint-bottomed chairs tilted back against the wall, chins on breasts, hats slouched over their faces, asleep . . . the great Mississippi, the majestic, the magnificent Mississippi, rolling its mile-wide tide along, shining in the sun.

SUCH IS THE MYTH, CAREFULLY CRAFTED BY CLEMENS HIMSELF, of the scene of the author's early life. The "white town drowsing" is of course Hannibal, Missouri, not the town of his birth at all (that honor belongs to the tiny hamlet of Florida, thirty miles away) but the growing river port town where John Marshall Clemens and Jane Lampton Clemens brought their five children in 1839.

Like many middle-class white Missourians, the family held enslaved people, selling all but one before moving to Hannibal. There they sold the last one remaining, a woman named Jenny, three years later. John Clemens was not a poor man—he was a lawyer able to buy property, concerned himself with civic improvements, and could put the title "judge" before his name after a stint as justice of the peace. He was prone to debt. Jane Lampton may have married John to spite a former lover, says Clemens, and she was more mischievous and livelier than her "dour, unloving" husband. Her red hair and ability to tell stories makes us think of her son; her love of dancing and horse riding gives a hint of her vivacity. "She cared for almost anything spectacular—parades, picnics, circuses, shows of all kinds," recalled a contemporary of Sam Clemens—it was Laura Hawkins, Sam's own Becky Thatcher, for whom the memory of this woman was vivid in 1928. And Jane Clemens's son could have been describing himself when he described her:

> *She was very bright, and was fond of banter and playful duels of wit, and she had a sort of ability which is rare in men and hardly existent in women—the ability to say a humorous thing with the perfect air of not knowing it to be humorous. Whenever I was in her presence, after I was grown, a battle of chaff was going on all the time, but under the guise of serious conversation.*

As a boy, Sam Clemens revisited the old Florida farm, now owned by an uncle, a place he said he could "call back" in old age: "I can call back the prairie, and its loneliness and peace, and a vast hawk hanging motionless in the sky, with his wings spread wide and the blue of the vault showing through the fringe of their end feathers." There he heard enslaved people tell ghost stories and picked up the art of storytelling. When he was eleven years old, his father died, and he remained in school only about a year more, until the schoolmaster left for the California Gold Rush. Clemens applied himself to life as a printer's apprentice. He took this skill to newspapers owned by his brother, Orion, and started writing humorous pieces to fill the

Jane Lampton Clemens was a brilliant storyteller, horsewoman, enjoyer of parties and circuses, and master of what Sam Clemens called "the chaff," a constant stream of banter with her son. Her influence on her son's work and high spirits was profound. THE MARK TWAIN HOUSE & MUSEUM COLLECTIONS.

Samuel Clemens took to sea in 1867 in what amounted to a Mediterranean cruise. He noted the peculiarities of his innocent fellow American travelers and their encounters with sophisticated Europeans, pillorying them both in funny and lyrical letters to the *Alta California* newspaper. The job of turning these letters into a book brought him to Hartford, where his publisher, Elisha Bliss, had his offices. THE MARK TWAIN HOUSE & MUSEUM. GIFT OF SAMUEL D. STEINBERG.

pages: "The Dandy Frightening the Squatter," a one-punch vindication of the frontier life, was the first piece that appeared outside his hometown, reprinted in Boston and Philadelphia journals. At age seventeen, he began a series of travels that belied his origins as a small-town boy, working as a typesetter in St. Louis, New York, and Philadelphia—and visiting Washington, stopping by Congress to see and hear some of the great political orators of the pre–Civil War period. His literary output consisted of "letters" to newspapers, under a wide variety of pseudonyms, a good soapbox for opinion couched in humorous terms. In 1857, as economic panic and religious revival swept America, he decided to seek his fortune in South America.

> *I had been reading about the recent exploration of the river Amazon by an expedition sent out by our government. It was said that*

the expedition, owing to difficulties, had not thoroughly explored a part of the country lying about the head-waters, some four thousand miles from the mouth of the river. It was only about fifteen hundred miles from Cincinnati to New Orleans, where I could doubtless get a ship. I had thirty dollars left; I would go and complete the exploration of the Amazon. This was all the thought I gave to the subject. I never was great in matters of detail.

But he got no farther than New Orleans, where he instead became an apprentice riverboat pilot: "I supposed that all a pilot had to do was to keep his boat in the river, and I did not consider that that could be much of a trick, since it was so wide." It took a lot more than that, as Clemens later described in *Life on the Mississippi*, that masterpiece of the kind of understated deadpan humor he had learned from his mother. Two years later, he got his pilot's license, which in an earlier era would have been the achievement of a dream and set him up for life, but the Civil War broke the Mississippi in two and, in 1861 (after a brief stint in a quasi-Confederate regiment), he left for Nevada with his brother Orion, who had campaigned hard for Abraham Lincoln and was appointed secretary to the governor of the Nevada Territory as a reward.

In Nevada, he staked silver claims that didn't pan out and picked up the habit of writing newspaper letters again; these won him a job for the Virginia City *Territorial Enterprise*. On February 3, 1863, he published the first of three letters using the name "Mark Twain." The following year, he decamped to San Francisco, evading a Nevada anti-dueling law, and wrote for papers there, spending some

On April 9, 1859, Samuel Clemens fulfilled a boyhood dream by becoming a licensed pilot on the Mississippi River. It's a job he might have stayed in for life if the Civil War had not intervened. THE MARINERS' MUSEUM AND PARK, NEWPORT NEWS, VIRGINIA.

"Jim Smiley and His Jumping Frog" was published in the *New York Saturday Press* in November 1865, a literary breakthrough for the writer only recently dubbed Mark Twain. The sketch shown was used to promote Clemens's lectures in which he related the tale. THE MARK TWAIN HOUSE & MUSEUM COLLECTIONS.

AMERICAN HUMOUR.

time in Calaveras County in the Gold Country near Sacramento. An odd story of a frog jumping contest, relayed to him by a bartender in Angel's Camp, was his ticket to fame—his version of it, "Jim Smiley and His Jumping Frog," appeared in the *New York Saturday Press* in 1865. He became a kind of traveling correspondent, first for the *Sacramento Union* and then the *Alta California* of San Francisco, which sent him east, where he saw the publication of his first book, *The Celebrated Jumping Frog of Calaveras County and Other Sketches*. He joined the passengers on the *Quaker City*, regarded as the first American cruise ship, in June 1867 on its passage from New York to the Holy Land via the Mediterranean and Black Seas, with some inland excursions. The *Alta* paid him $1,250 for his passage and $20 for each letter, of which there were fifty-three. His dispatches to the *Alta* (along with six to the *New York Tribune* and three to the *New York Herald*) were widely read, and when he returned in November, a publisher from Hartford, Connecticut—Elisha Bliss of the American Publishing Company—was among those who wanted to turn them into a book. At the same time, he wrote to his mother, "Am pretty well known, now—intend to be better known."

Clemens liked Bliss's proposition, which ultimately brought him to Hartford for several visits in 1868. He was still sending letters to the *Alta* and sent its readers his impressions:

> *I have been here several days. Of all the beautiful towns it has been my fortune to see this is the chief. It is a city of 40,000*

inhabitants, and seems to be composed almost entirely of dwelling houses—not single-shaped affairs, stood on end and packed together like a "deck" of cards, but massive private hotels, scattered along the broad, straight streets, from fifty all the way up to two hundred yards apart. Each house sits in the midst of about an acre of green grass, or flower beds or ornamental shrubbery, guarded on all sides by the trimmest hedges of arbor-vitae, and by files of huge forest trees that cast a shadow like a thunder-cloud. Some of these stately dwellings are almost buried from sight in parks and forests of these noble trees. Everywhere the eye turns it is blessed with a vision of refreshing green. You do not know what beauty is if you have not been here.

LIVY

So began Clemens's affection for this old trading town on the Connecticut River. But at the same time that he was falling in love with Hartford, he was falling in love with Olivia Louise Langdon. Livy, ten years younger than he was, had grown up in Elmira, New York, three hundred miles from Hartford but not at all distant in terms of atmosphere, consanguinity, and religion. In a house that could be called as much a private hotel as any in the Connecticut capital, Olivia Langdon suffered from ill health and developed a love for reading. She read prodigiously, in a serious way that her daughter Susy later described as "studying." Her commonplace book recorded not only Shakespeare, Milton, and Austen but also contemporaries Margaret Fuller, Thomas Carlyle, and Henry David Thoreau—as well as John Ruskin, whose works were having a strong influence on the architects who were to build the Hartford house. She was often described as "frail," but she could give as good as she got, even when it came to Samuel Clemens. She called him "Youth" because of his ebullience, and he called her "Gravity" because she brought him down to earth.

Several years later, when they were a married couple, she provided a good example of this quality. Livy had written a letter to a friend, and Samuel had added to it, rather pompously clarifying a point. Under his comment, she wrote her own: "How thankful I am that you have some one to interpret my letter for you. L." He wrote under that, "It is a form of grammar that renders interpretation very necessary. S." And the dialogue went on:

I don't think so—because—L.

And I do for the same reason. S.

No.—L.

Go to bed, Woman! S.

I am not sleepy—L.

This it is to be married. S.

Yes indeed—woe is me! This it is to be married. L.

Go on—jaw-jaw-jaw. S.

I don't think so—L.

Well. Take the last word. S.

Livy may have derived the spirit that made Mark Twain her foil from her unusual parents, who had deep abolitionist opinions and great wealth. Jervis Langdon controlled lumber forests and mines from Nova Scotia to western Pennsylvania. They subscribed to a liberal, socially conscious form of Congregationalism practiced by the Reverend Thomas Beecher and helped him build a church that doubled as a social hall and community center, offering free baths, a lending library, and billiards to the city's poor. As abolitionists, they were close friends with the great African American author and statesman Frederick Douglass. And they had connections with Hartford and Clemens's own past: the Reverend Beecher, a Connecticut native, was brother to the extraordinary Beecher sisters who included Harriet Beecher Stowe, educator Catharine Beecher, and women's rights pioneer Isabella Beecher Hooker. Hooker's daughter Alice was a close friend of Livy's. A brother was the Reverend Henry Ward Beecher, the powerful abolitionist preacher who had organized the *Quaker City* trip.

As a result of this Elmira–Hartford connection, one of the passengers on the trip was Livy's brother, Charles Langdon, who, as Clemens tells it, showed

The Wild Humorist of the Pacific Slope and the wealthy Elmira, New York, heiress Olivia Langdon, "Livy," were ten years apart in age when they were married in February 1870. She was twenty-four; he was thirty-four. After a year of living in Buffalo, New York, they had Hartford firmly in mind as the place where they wanted to build a home. (LEFT) THE MARK TWAIN HOUSE & MUSEUM. GIFT OF OLIVIA LADA-MOCARSKI. (RIGHT) THE MARK TWAIN HOUSE & MUSEUM. GIFT OF THE HARPERS.

him a miniature portrait on ivory of his sister as the ship lay at anchor in the Bay of Smyrna, off Turkey. Clemens was instantly in love but didn't meet the object of his romantic devotion and future bantering until December 1867, when he accompanied the Langdons to hear Charles Dickens read from *David Copperfield* at Steinway Hall in New York City. Still writing his dispatches to the *Alta California*, Clemens was critical: "He is a bad reader, in one sense—because he does not enunciate his words sharply and distinctly—he does not cut the syllables cleanly, and therefore many and many of them fell dead before they reached our part of the house." But he found the real value in the evening in Livy's company: "It made the fortune of my life—not in dollars, I am not thinking in dollars; it made the real fortune of my life in that it made the happiness of my life."

Clemens's serious courtship of Livy Langdon began in the summer of 1868, immediately after he delivered the manuscript of *The Innocents Abroad* to

Bliss in Hartford. It continued for a year and a half through initial refusal and a careful vetting of the proposed groom by the Langdons. At last, the two were married in the Elmira home on February 2, 1870, as Beecher shared the ceremony with a new Hartford friend, the Reverend Joseph Twichell of Asylum Hill Congregational Church. Twichell, an affable and sociable Yale graduate and war veteran, was revered among his well-heeled parishioners in the western end of the city and had quickly become a fast friend to Clemens.

The Clemenses started out married life in Buffalo, New York, in a home and with a newspaper job for Samuel provided by his new father-in-law. Their first child, Langdon Clemens, was born there on November 7. But their life in Buffalo (Clemens called it "that loathsome place") was marred by the death of Jervis Langdon, a breakdown in Livy's health, and the death of one of her old classmates while on a visit to the Clemenses. Less than a year later, the couple pulled up stakes and moved to Hartford, leasing a house from John and Isabella Hooker. There they would be surrounded by new friends like Twichell and old ones like Alice Hooker, now Alice Hooker Day. They would enjoy the stimulation and the joys of a close-knit literary community in a prosperous city, quickly joining the circle of writers, editors, lawyers, divines, and businessmen who made up an unusual neighborhood, Nook Farm.

CHAPTER TWO

"That Birth-Place of Six-Shooters"

HARRIET BEECHER STOWE WAS PROBABLY THE most famous writer in the world when she moved to Hartford in 1864 and described its comfortable, bourgeois aspect: "Old Hartford seems fat, rich and cozy—stocks higher than ever, business plenty—everything as tranquil as possible." The city had prospered since the days when it supplied woolen clothing for Revolutionary soldiers, broadening from merchant-banker city to a manufacturing center to a place that supplied insurance to the nation. It was a maelstrom of enterprise, epitomized in the title of a sermon directed to the businessmen of Hartford by the Reverend Horace Bushnell, a liberal theologian and civic reformer: "Prosperity Our Duty." The Aetna Fire Insurance Company had been formed in 1819 by the grandfather of J. P. Morgan, the financial titan, and the effect was monumental. Insurance was still king in Clemens's and Stowe's day. The year after the Clemenses wed in Elmira, the city of Chicago burned, and Marshall Jewell of Hartford's appropriately named Phoenix Fire Insurance Company was on hand to settle claims over a barrelhead before the embers cooled.

The city's wealth became so great in the 1870s that the editor of the *Hartford Daily Courant*, Charles Hopkins Clark, produced figures in *Scribner's Monthly* magazine that he said proved that the city produced more wealth per capita than any other city in the United States. The insurance companies' new mansard-roofed headquarters lined the principal streets; the mansions of their owners and managers lined Farmington Avenue. The manufacturers thrived as well: the blue onion dome of the Colt factory rose over the South Meadows as workmen created revolvers and Gatling guns below it, and Jewell's great leather belting enterprise provided a means to transfer the motive power from stationary steam engines to factory machinery all over America.

A string of horse-drawn cabs is lined up on Main Street in front of the grounds of the Old State House, with the spire of the Center Congregational Church, founded in 1635, providing a suitably old New England focus to the city. THE MARK TWAIN HOUSE & MUSEUM COLLECTIONS.

Pratt & Whitney produced machine parts, and the great Cheney silk mills of nearby Manchester reeled out yards and yards of the smooth, slinky, desirable material. None of these devclopments were lost on Clemens during his first visits to the city in 1868:

> Hartford dollars have a place in half the great moneyed enterprises in the Union. All those Phoenix and Charter Oak Insurance Companies, whose gorgeous chromo-lithographic show-cards it has been my delight to study in far away cities, are located here. The Sharp's rifle factory is here; the great silk factory of this section is here; the heaviest subscription publication houses in the land are here; and the last, and greatest, the Colt's revolver manufactory is a Hartford institution. Some friends went with me to see the revolver establishment. It comprises a great range of tall brick buildings, and on every floor is a dense wilderness of strange iron machines that stretches away into remote distances and confusing perspectives—a tangled forest of rods, bars, pulleys, wheels,

> *and all the imaginable and unimaginable forms of mechanism...*
> *I took a living interest in that birth-place of six-shooters, because*
> *I had seen so many graceful specimens of their performances in*
> *the deadfalls of Washoe and California.*

"Then," he asked rhetorically in an *Alta* letter, "where are the poor of Hartford? I confess I do not know. They are 'corralled,' doubtless—corralled in some unsanctified corner of this paradise whither my feet have not yet wandered, I suppose."

It was not long before he found one of many such unsanctified corners. Just a few days after he made the acquaintance of the energetic young clergyman Joe Twichell, the two of them made their way to the city almshouse—a city residence for the poor—at the edge of the city. There, he wrote Livy, he helped Twichell "preach & sing to the inmates. (I helped in the singing, anyhow.)"

The condition of these residents of fat, cozy Hartford shocked Clemens.

> *Heaven & earth, what a sight it was! Cripples, jibbering idiots, raving madmen; thieves, rowdies, paupers; little children, stone blind; blind men & women; old, old, men & women, with that sad absent look in their faces that tells of thoughts that are busy with "the days that are no more." I have not had anything touch me so since I saw the leper hospitals of Honolulu & Damascus.*

Three weeks later, Twichell took Clemens to New Haven, to his alma mater, Yale. There "the Wild Humorist of the Pacific Slope" became an honorary member of the secret society Scroll and Key. The contrast of concern for the poor and distressed and enjoyment of privilege was to be a constant theme in Clemens's life.

(Opposite page) A horse-drawn trolley makes its way along Farmington Avenue through the aftermath of a New England snowstorm during the time the Clemenses lived in the neighborhood. Clemens, on an early visit, described the houses in the area as "private hotels." THE MARK TWAIN HOUSE & MUSEUM. GIFT OF MRS. WALTER PRATT.

(This page) The Connecticut Mutual Life Insurance Company displays its wedding-cake architecture on Hartford's Main Street. Clemens wrote, "All those Phoenix and Charter Oak Insurance Companies, whose gorgeous chromo-lithographic show-cards it has been my delight to study in far away cities, are located here." THE MARK TWAIN HOUSE & MUSEUM COLLECTIONS.

NOOK FARM

On the western side of the city, south of the almshouse and west of the Sharps rifle plant, was a semi-wooded rural paradise. A hundred-acre farm had been bought up by two prominent lawyers in town who happened to be brothers-in-law: John Hooker, the brilliant husband of Isabella and a founder of the state Republican Party, and Francis Gillette, who, during a brief stint as a U.S. senator before the war, came close to being lynched by a pro-slavery mob in the streets of Washington. Like almost all prominent Hartford businessmen, they had interests in the city's insurance companies.

They wished to populate the farm where they resided—Gillette and family originally in the old farmhouse, the Hookers in a brand-new, brick Gothic Revival house—with like-minded members of the liberal Republican abolitionist middle class. So they sold plots during the war to like-minded men such as Charles Dudley Warner, wartime editor of the *Hartford Evening Press*; its publisher, Civil War general Joseph Hawley; and, the doyenne of them all, Harriet Beecher Stowe, the author of *Uncle Tom's Cabin, or Life Among the Lowly*, and her husband, Professor Calvin Stowe. They called this new neighborhood Nook Farm because it lay in a bend, or "nook," in the Little River (or Park River, or Hog River) that flowed south on the western side of the community. Its heart was along Forest Street, which ran south from Farmington Avenue, one of the main routes from downtown Hartford to the west. John Hooker described the feeling of the place: "The early comers were generally family or personal friends, and we lived like a little society by ourselves—each of us making free of the others' houses, and each keeping open house." Warner later put the neighborhood into a novel; a home there "commanded a view of city spires and towers on the one hand, and on the other of a broken country of clustering trees and cottages, rising toward a range of hills which showed purple and warm against the pale straw-color of the winter sunsets."

It was to this sociable, bucolic place that Samuel and Livy Clemens, with ten-month-old Langdon, came to lease the Hooker house on October 1, 1871. The ex-Confederate was determined to become a New Englander. "Making friends in Yankee land is a slow, slow business, but they are friends worth having when they are made," he wrote to his brother, Orion. The couple had a copy of the Reverend Bushnell's *Christian Nurture*, a manual for child-rearing with a forward-looking religious tinge; this tome was to help them raise Langdon and the new baby they were expecting. And Livy already had her eye on a piece of land where they might build a house.

CHAPTER THREE

"They Preferred Mr. Potter to Everyone Else"

IN MARCH 1871, WHEN THE CLEMENSES HAD MOVED out of the Buffalo house to stay in Livy's family home in Elmira, they already had in mind that they would buy property and build in Hartford. "We are selling our dwelling & everything here & are going to spend the summer in Elmira while we build a house in Hartford. Eight months' sickness & death in one place is enough," Clemens wrote to a friend.

The summer came and went. In October, they moved into the Hookers' home. (This building still stands behind apartment buildings at the nearby corner of Forest and Hawthorn Streets, providing Hartford with two Mark Twain houses.) Samuel Clemens almost immediately set off on a lecture tour, a prime source of family income in those days. Livy, about four months pregnant, took the opportunity to examine a wooded hillside above the Little River. Below it, enclosed by a loop of the narrow stream, she saw a pasture; beyond this to the west, meadows interrupted by occasional clusters of houses and steeples stretched toward the heights of Talcott Mountain on the horizon. They purchased it from a local attorney, Franklin Chamberlin, who, despite Hooker's and Gillette's attempts to populate Nook Farm with amenable folk, didn't seem to have been well liked. It was an odd, narrow, steep sliver of land on which to build a house.

Plans were set aside for a year during which Clemens published *Roughing It*, a fantastic account of his travels west with Orion on a stagecoach and what he found in Nevada and California. The book includes memorable descriptions of a Pony Express rider and a coyote, tales of prospecting, the anticipation of

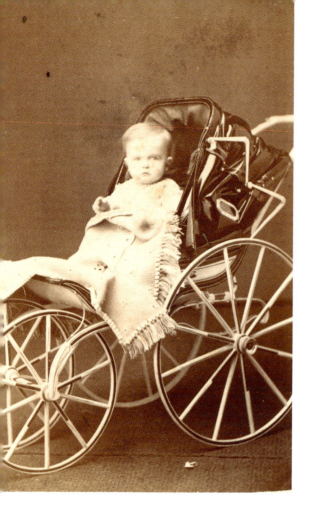

Though the Clemenses were happy to be among their new neighbors and friends in the intellectual fellowship of Nook Farm, tragedy followed them. Slow to develop, son Langdon Clemens contracted diphtheria and died in the spring of 1872. THE MARK TWAIN HOUSE & MUSEUM COLLECTIONS.

fortune, and the instant loss of it; a vivid portrait of the moon landscape of Mono Lake; and wild tales of Western lore, such as one in which a landslide that put one man's land on top of another's prompted a complex real estate lawsuit. The book was published in February 1872; the Clemenses' first daughter, Olivia Susan Clemens, was born in March. Then, in June, another tragedy of the kind the Clemenses had been trying to flee: Langdon, at nineteen months, died of diphtheria. Clemens blamed the boy's death on himself—for being too lost in thought during a carriage ride to notice that the blankets had shifted off the child. He threw himself into work on the Connecticut shore and then traveled to England to see to the publication of The Innocents Abroad and to plan a book about the English. In the fall, he started work on his first novel, The Gilded Age: A Tale of Today, collaborating with neighbor Charles Dudley Warner, with Livy Clemens and Susan Warner as its first editors—the authors read each day's work to them in the evenings.

Charles's brother, George Warner, and his wife, Lilly—a daughter of Francis Gillette—were also moving into the leafy Nook Farm glades. George traveled a great deal in his job with the Emigrant Aid Society, which was helping settle newly arrived immigrants from Sweden and Germany in places like Iowa and Wisconsin. The couple left a set of delightfully detailed and sometimes catty correspondence about the doings and denizens of Nook Farm. On a trip to New York, George Warner admired a townhouse on Thirty-Seventh Street that the architect Edward Tuckerman Potter, already known for church-building work in the Hartford area, had constructed for a patron. The Warners were not wealthy but engaged Potter to build their home on Forest Street, just a little south of the land that Livy had her eye on. The Warner house was in progress while the Clemenses pondered their building plans, and George and Lilly became their advisors in this effort. George wrote to Lilly that he had asked Potter for a

454

A noisy & rather ill-natured debate followed, now, & lasted hour after hour. The friends of the bill were instructed by the leaders to <u>make no effort to check this</u>; it was deemed better strategy to tire out the opposition; it was decided to vote down every proposition to adjourn, & so continue the sitting into the night; opponents might desert, then, one by one & weaken their party, for they had no personal stake in the bill. [It was getting toward the end of the session, now, & the rule which adjourned the House at a customary hour had been suspended to make way for the night sittings that must]

During the Clemenses' early years in Hartford, when they were living on Forest Street in a rented house, author and neighbor Charles Dudley Warner collaborated on a novel of Washington intrigue, melodrama, and crooked Western land deals. Published in 1873, it was a heady mixture, then and now. In its title, they coined a phrase that described an era for all time—the Gilded Age.

THE MARK TWAIN HOUSE & MUSEUM COLLECTIONS.

Potter designed the home of the Clemenses' neighbors, George and Lilly Warner, who lobbied heavily to get the newcomers to use Potter for their own home. The press described such homes as being "in the English style." THE MARK TWAIN HOUSE & MUSEUM COLLECTIONS.

hand-colored photograph of the New York townhouse to show the Clemenses. He continued: "I wrote him yesterday to send it to you for the purpose of influencing the Clemenses about their house... I want immensely to get that house for Potter." (Potter seems to have given the Warners a break on their debt to him, perhaps in gratitude for their help in getting the Clemenses' work.)

In January 1873, another trip to England was planned, this time with Livy. Clemens wrote to a friend, with all the pride of a man still mildly amazed that he could live on his writing, that he had bought a piece of land from Chamberlin with a frontage of 544 feet on Farmington Avenue and "paid for it with first six months of 'Roughing It'—how's that?" He wrote another friend about the property

Lilly Warner was a strongly opinionated woman who relayed the tale of the Clemenses' house and its planning to her husband George, who traveled often on business. She walked the steep ground of the Clemenses' new property with Livy Clemens, talking over which way the front door should face, among other issues. "Mr. Clemens knew nothing about houses on paper & she must talk with somebody about it," Lilly reported.
COURTESY OF THE HARRIET BEECHER STOWE CENTER.

purchase: "I . . . shall have a house built in the midst of it while we are absent in England—& then we'll have a blow-out there every time you can run down from Boston."

He loved walking their new property, Livy reported: "Mr. Clemens seems to glory in his sense of possession; he goes daily into the lot, has had several falls trying to lay off the land by sliding around on his feet." Lilly and Livy also walked the ground with sketchbook in hand. Lilly wrote to George, "She came yesterday to show me her plan—drawn roughly 'because Mr. Clemens knew nothing about houses on paper & she must talk with somebody about it as she went along.'"

One thing Livy talked about with Lilly was which way the house would face. Because of the narrowness of the property, stretching as it did south from Farmington Avenue, it could not gracefully face that thoroughfare but had to face east or west—east, toward Forest Street and the backs of other Nook Farm homes, or west over the river, looking toward the distant hills. Facing west, Lilly opined, would be "queer & not the thing." But if it faced east, the utilitarian parts of the house—the kitchen, a planned dressing room—would get all the best views of the river and hills. As they walked along the crest of the hill, Lilly counseled professional aid: "I told her I shouldn't try to get it right myself, for an architect could see at once how to do it & would make suggestions which she would never think of being so unused to the business." Livy agreed and said "they preferred Mr. Potter to everyone else."

EDWARD TUCKERMAN POTTER

When the era in which Edward Tuckerman Potter designed and built houses and churches was looked back on from the perspective of the 1930s, architectural critic Lewis Mumford spoke of the "morass of jerry-building, tedious archaism, and spurious romanticism that made up the architectural achievement of the nineteenth century." This was the jumble of styles that an earlier critic had called the "Victorian Cathartic, the Tubercular or Queen Anne Style, and the Cataleptic Style." Mumford and others saw the 1870s as the last gasp of a period in decline before the advent of a new age, which would be personified in the work of architect Henry Hobson Richardson. In the next decade, Richardson built massive structures of Romanesque arches and subtly colored stone that had a formal unity, despite their size. (Though his greatest buildings are elsewhere, a Richardson marvel, the Brown Thomson Building on Main Street, is located a brief bus ride from the Mark Twain House.) In the architectural succession viewed by Mumford, from Richardson's influence grew the achievements of Louis Sullivan, the "father of the modern skyscraper," and the great residential work of Frank Lloyd Wright.

Even Potter's biographer, Sarah Bradford Landau, has conceded that "American High Gothic buildings were generally looked upon as anomalous and even freakish until the 1960s." Potter, of course, had no idea he was part of a stale and passing tradition, feeling rather that he was on the cutting edge of things.

Born in Schenectady, New York, in 1831, he was the son of an Episcopal clergyman who became bishop of the diocese of Pennsylvania when Potter was a teenager. Potter attended Union College in Schenectady and then apprenticed for two years with the leader of the American Gothic Revival in church architecture, Richard Upjohn. Both Potter and Upjohn were members of a generation of young artists, designers, and architects who rebelled against the classicism and symmetry of the buildings of the time as well as the ugliness of the era's factories and cramped workers' housing. John Ruskin, the English art critic, had sparked this movement. He saw in the medieval Gothic style not only aesthetic but also moral superiority to the Greek and Roman models that had been followed since the Renaissance and a relief from modern capitalist philistinism:

> *And when that fallen Roman, in the utmost impotence of his luxury, and insolence of his guilt, became the model for the imitation of civilized Europe, at the close of the so-called Dark ages, the*

> *word Gothic became a term of unmitigated contempt, not unmixed with aversion. From that contempt, by the exertion of the antiquaries and architects of this century, Gothic architecture has been sufficiently vindicated. . . . I believe it is in this very character that it deserves our profoundest reverence.*

In the United States, Upjohn was among those inspired by such words. He joined the group of mainly English church architects who called themselves "ecclesiologists." Ruskin's inspiration shows in Upjohn's great Gothic Revival masterpieces in New York, including Trinity Church in Lower Manhattan, completed in 1846, a decade before Potter became his apprentice. (Upjohn's son later submitted the winning design for the present Connecticut State Capitol.) A job with Upjohn was a plum, and Potter seems to have thrived under the master's tutelage.

Both master and apprentice had deep connections to the Episcopal Church. Not only was Potter's father a bishop, but so were his uncle and, ultimately, his brother. His grandfather, Eliphalet Nott, an inventor of steamboats and stoves, had been president of Union College since 1804. These connections led to Edward being asked, at age twenty-eight, to design a large central Alumni Hall for the center of the circular-plan Union campus. The money ran out for this vast building, ultimately called Nott Memorial, but Potter finished the job in his prime in 1877. It survives today, a sixteen-sided, domed building of bluestone, sandstone, and Vermont slate with tall windows and patterned masonry that give it the air of a Persian mosque.

Potter's first major church design was also in Schenectady: the First Dutch Reformed Church, a building on a difficult corner lot, to be topped by a tower and spire and capable of seating eight hundred people. It was a triumph of light and carved detail. "From the beginning of his career Potter was concerned with providing adequate light in his buildings and with the quality of that light," biographer Landau has written. In the Mark Twain House, the light coming through the clerestory window—a row of windows built into the roof above the top of the stairwell—is a purely ecclesiological device.

In the 1860s, Potter built many churches but also—thanks to the nexus of prominent Episcopalians who recommended his work and a general passion for Gothic buildings—moved into residential design. It was one of the townhouses he built for the Brown family on Thirty-Seventh Street in Manhattan that caught the Warners' eye when they were planning a Nook Farm home. But

Until interest in Victorian architecture revived in the 1960s, Potter and his mentor, Richard Upjohn, were considered part of a generally forgettable school of architecture from which emerged pioneers like Henry Hobson Richardson. Richardson's Cheney block (*above*) on Hartford's Main Street was built in 1875–1876 and is considered a precursor of his more famous Marshall Field building in Chicago a decade later. THE MARK TWAIN HOUSE & MUSEUM COLLECTIONS.

Potter also, early in his career, had received a commission from Susan Hall, a prominent patron of the church in Muncy, Pennsylvania, who asked him to build a country home.

Potter designed a house for Hall in 1861 that appears, according to a watercolor reproduction in Landau's biography of the architect, to be a miniature, slightly blurred version of the Clemens home. Its Jacobean-style chimneys rise over steeply sloping roofs. A broad porch stretches along the front right of the house—the end of the porch hidden by trees, but you can almost picture the extended porch, or *ombra*, of the later building. A small, almost separate structure offset to one side mirrors the Clemenses' semi-detached kitchen wing. There are no vast gables in the Hall house like the flared Elizabethan pair that loom over the entry of the Clemens house in Hartford, but otherwise these are definitely kissing cousins.

Potter had been circling Hartford around the time the Warners found him—he had built a small Episcopal church in East Hartford and was at work on a larger one in Wethersfield, south of the city. But his most prominent local job was the Church of the Good Shepherd, commissioned by Elizabeth Colt, the wealthy widow of the six-shooter manufacturer whose factory and firearms had so impressed Clemens. The elaborate spired church Potter built for Colt in Hartford's South Meadows even portrayed, in stone-carved bas-relief, the six-shooters that created the family wealth. So, when the Warners hired him and passed along their recommendation to the Clemenses, they knew they were passing along quality.

Potter set to work in the spring of 1873. The Clemens family displayed a glorious lack of concern about what was happening on the narrow Hartford hillside, leaving almost immediately for a planned long vacation in England. They probably saw only a preliminary perspective of the house that Potter had produced, showing a three-story brick building with its two large, flared gables above and on either side of the entrance. The entry was protected under a protruding *porte cochère*, which would allow for entry and exit from carriages on rainy Hartford spring days. Just as Lilly Warner had recommended to Livy, the entry

Edward Tuckerman Potter's most prominent structure in Hartford prior to his design of the Clemens home was the Church of the Good Shepherd, part of the vast Colt factory and residential complex in the city's South Meadows. Built for Samuel Colt's widow, Elizabeth Colt, it represented the arms maker's trade in stone relief on the south porch—crossed six-shooters.
THE MARK TWAIN HOUSE & MUSEUM COLLECTIONS.

The Clemenses arranged for Potter to design and build their house and then promptly left for a long European vacation, leaving the details of construction and contractors in the hands of their attorney. It's likely that the one visual clue to what would be built for them was this architectural view by Potter in the archives of The Mark Twain House & Museum, which, with minor exceptions, mirrors the eventual reality. THE MARK TWAIN HOUSE & MUSEUM COLLECTIONS.

faced east, toward the backs of the Forest Street neighbors' homes. A fabulous turret topped a balcony outside the second-floor master bedroom, and the roofline displayed the jut of three ornate Jacobean chimneys.

The problem Lilly Warner had noted about placing the kitchen on the hillside side of the house—that the servants in the kitchen would have the best view west toward Talcott Mountain—had been solved. The kitchen and servants' room above it had been placed, as in the Susan Hall house, in an almost detached wing extending north. This wing had a blank wall facing the avenue, which might have been expected to be the side where the entrance to the whole house should be. This semi-detached wing was accessible from the upper stories of the main house by an enclosed, roofed exterior staircase whose angle downward and varied brick patterns provide one of the most interesting visual details of the sketch, like a stair in a medieval castle courtyard. And, if Livy and Samuel saw it in black and white (like the sketch that survives in The Mark Twain House & Museum archives today), they saw only a hint of the polychromatic brick in "shape and position, straight and askew" that is such a noticeable feature of the home in its present-day restored state.

With the image of their future home in mind, the Clemens family left on May 17 for a four-month trip partly involved in gathering items for the house—they made a jaunt to Paris, and in Scotland they obtained a massive carved chimneypiece from the castle of the Mitchell–Innes family in Ayton, Berwickshire. They returned November 2, but Clemens set sail again six days later to see to the English copyright for *The Gilded Age* and to give a series of lectures based on his stories from *Roughing It*. He suffered the pangs of distance from Livy (now pregnant again) and Susy and breathed uncomfortably in the smothering coal-smoke fog of London.

Back in Hartford, Potter was assisted by a junior partner, Alfred H. Thorp, who has been seen as the French connection by scholars trying to puzzle together the multiple influences on the Clemens home. Thorp had studied in Paris with the renowned architect Pierre Jérôme Honoré Daumet. So had Robert Peabody, who designed a house in Newport two years earlier that also bore a striking resemblance to the Clemens home, down to the slight flare of the roofline on the gables and the crisscross railings on the extensive porches. Another model, says scholar Richard Chafee, might have been a villa in Berlin portrayed in an architectural journal that Potter is known to have pored over. But while the details of these structures evoke the eventual details of the Clemens home, the one house recognizably similar is the humbler Susan Hall house in Pennsylvania.

The Clemenses were back in Hartford in January and were able to see progress on the house. Livy went over the building with Lilly Warner, who commented, "What an immense house it seems. That billiard room is beautiful. I like it all as I see it in my mind furnished with soft carpets and other things." A workman on the house recalled, "Mr. and Mrs. Clemens were accustomed to come over daily from the Hooker place at Hawthorne and Forest Streets, their temporary home." He remembered the pregnant Livy being reluctant to climb the stairs, but he had seen "Mark Twain pick her up in his arms and gaily mount the stairs, the pair laughing and chiding one another."

The Clemenses did not intend to occupy the house until fall, after they made their customary summer visit to Elmira—this time to be made memorable by the birth of their second daughter, Clara. "Mrs. C. gets along very, very slowly," Clemens wrote to a friend. "But a week hence, if she can travel, we'll leave for Elmira. I must get her away from house & building cares. She don't sleep worth a cent."

They left on April 15, two weeks sooner than planned, which may have been why Clemens's friend Mary Mason Fairbanks had to use Potter as a guide when she came to Hartford. Many pages back we left the visitor and the architect standing on the porch, but now it's time to go inside.

CHAPTER FOUR
A Tour of the House

THE FIRST FLOOR

"Here," said he, as we stood in the main hall from which opened parlors, library, and dining-rooms, "here we must produce pleasant effects, so here we put this fire-place, which shall have its antique tiles and its polished andirons. Over the mantel we have put a window opposite, and yet more, the outer landscape of Farmington Avenue and the country beyond."

—Mary Mason Fairbanks, 1874

The Entry Hall

Fairbanks and Potter entered the house through a narrow entrance hall with one door to the left and another to the right; the left-hand door led to a small reception room, where a visitor might remove a coat or shawl, and the right-hand door to a bright drawing room, where a guest would be received and entertained. Ahead of them the entry broadened to a larger room at the base of a rising staircase. The walk in must have been a little cramped, and the walls were quite plainly decorated. But on our tour, we have the advantage of time travel and more than 150 years over Fairbanks. The Clemenses wrought changes to this entry, and then others changed it further, and then the room was painstakingly restored. Today we see the house not in 1874 but as it looked roughly a decade later, and that makes a difference.

The reception room is gone, its corners marked by spiral dark, wooden columns, and the entry hall is now broad and high, with the sparkle of thousands of tiny triangles of iridescent paint. Wooden moldings in starlike patterns divide the space on the ceilings. The effect is like seeing mother-of-pearl laid into the wood; the lighting is dim, to simulate gas lighting. The flickering lamps would have made the room a shimmering marvel. The decorative work is by a firm with a famous name attached: Louis C. Tiffany & Co., Associated Artists, a group of partners Tiffany (the son of the famous jeweler) brought together for

The entry hall evokes sharp intakes of breath from those who enter. Although it's dark, the height of the room, sweeping up into the tall staircase, and the splendor of stenciling added in 1881, evoking silver or mother-of-pearl, gives the feeling of a Persian palace or a Moroccan mosque. THE MARK TWAIN HOUSE & MUSEUM. PHOTOGRAPH BY JOHN GROO.

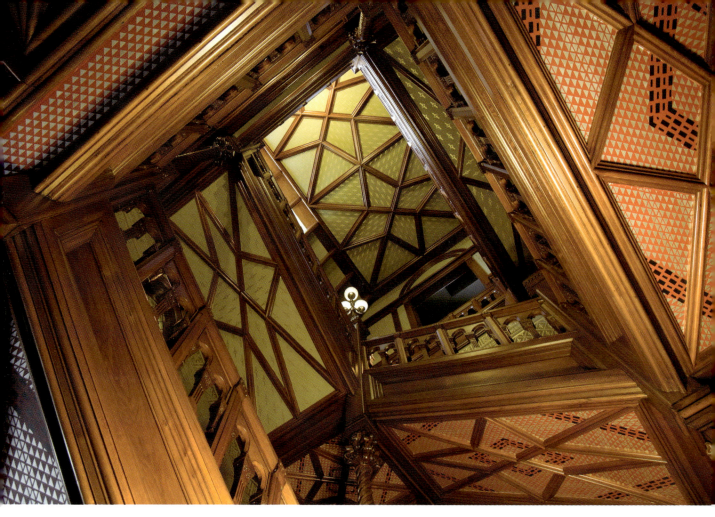

At the bottom of the staircase, visitors look up, and they were meant to. The banisters and balustrades were distorted slightly in perspective to make the stairwell appear even higher and grander than it actually is. THE MARK TWAIN HOUSE & MUSEUM. PHOTOGRAPH BY JOHN GROO.

a few years in the late 1870s and early 1880s. (We'll hear more of this work, accomplished in 1881, when we return to the Clemenses' history in the house.) We see heavy, dark furniture; a colossal staircase rising to the upper reaches of the house; a fireplace with a glass window over it; and, in the corner, an 1884 bust of Mark Twain by a Clemens protégé, Karl Gerhardt. ("If you run across anybody who wants a bust, be sure & recommend Gerhardt on my say-so," Clemens wrote to a friend.)

Just as Mary Fairbanks described it in 1874, the rooms fan out from this central hall—the library, the dining room, and the drawing room. The window Potter refers to over the mantel still carries light from Farmington Avenue into this entry, which is otherwise dark—as contemporaries, including Livy Clemens herself, noted. "I felt again distressed by the darkness of the hall," she wrote one summer, "but decided to wait and see just how it is in winter when the vines are off." A writer for *Harper's* magazine called the window over the

It's not the original, but the music box in the front entry hall stands in for the one Clemens bought in Geneva during a grand writing tour—and shopping spree—that he and Livy undertook in 1878–1879. A concert by this machine, owned by a Clemens contemporary who also lived in the Nook Farm neighborhood, included bells struck by tiny brass birds. THE MARK TWAIN HOUSE & MUSEUM. PHOTOGRAPHS BY JOHN GROO.

mantel, the flue divided to pass around it, a "large plate glass suggesting Alice's Adventures"—that is, her passage into Looking Glass Land in *Through the Looking Glass*. A window is there today, where visitors to the Mark Twain House sometimes turn to check their hair before realizing they are looking into another room.

These visitors proceed, as Mary Fairbanks did, on a tour led by a historical interpreter who not only imparts a wealth of information about Samuel and Livy Clemens and their household but also evokes responses and reactions from those they guide. Through the special tours of the museum's Living History program, they might be guided by members of the household acting in character: Livy Clemens, daughter Susy, coachman Patrick McAleer, housemaid Lizzie

Wills, family friend Reverend Joseph Twichell, or two of the most significant members of the household—butler George Griffin and lady's maid Katy Leary.

Griffin would most likely have greeted a front-door visitor to the house during the Clemens era. He had been born enslaved in Maryland and, having either secured his own freedom or been liberated by the Union army, served as body servant during the Civil War to General Charles Devens Jr. of Boston, later attorney general in the Hayes administration. Griffin came north after the war and worked as a waiter at the Allyn Hotel in Hartford but also took occasional odd jobs—one of which was washing the windows for the Clemenses; hired on permanently, he stayed with the family for eighteen years.

"There was nothing commonplace about George," Clemens wrote. "He had a remarkably good head; his promise was good, his note was good; he could be trusted to any extent with money or other valuables; his word was worth par, when he was not protecting Mrs. Clemens or the family interests or furnishing information about a horse to a person he was proposing to get a bet out of." He was an "idol to the children" and "would postpone work any time to join the children in their play if invited, for he was very strong, & always ready for service as horse, camel, elephant or any other kind of transportation required." The butler once faced down a burglar with a pistol, which got him immortalized as "G. G., Chief of Ordnance" in a brief preface to *Adventures of Huckleberry Finn*. Griffin would require a visitor to wait on the divan, or on one of the heavy carved chairs that flanked the fireplace, and carry a *carte de visite* up to Mr. or Mrs. Clemens. If the visitor passed muster—on to the drawing room.

The Drawing Room

The contrast from the entry is remarkable—light is everywhere in this room, magnified by a mirror that reaches almost to the ceiling. Light-colored upholstery on the chairs and settee gives the place an airy feel after the heaviness of the hall. It's a room that seems linked to the Clemenses because so many items owned by them and used here are present. Many furnishings in the house were sold or dispersed over the years, and only some have found their way back; many have been replaced by nineteenth-century items that duplicate what was lost. A survivor is the chandelier in the center of the room; it was given to the Wadsworth Atheneum, Hartford's great art museum, by a later owner of the house and was ultimately returned. The same applies to the floor-to-ceiling mirror against the front wall of the room: a wedding present from the Langdons to the married couple, it was ultimately retrieved, its woodwork covered with paint, from a Hartford upholstery shop. Clara recalled watching her feet in this mirror during dancing lessons, though she and Susy would much rather have spent time "with our turtles, squirrels, dogs, and cats." The low armchair, side chairs, and settee belonged to the Clemenses, and the bust of Livy as a girl in the corner was in the Langdon home in Elmira. The Steinway piano was not theirs; neither was the great painting, a copy of *The Holy Family* by Andrea Del Sarto. But, like many better-off American tourists on European trips, they picked up copies of Old Masters like this one.

Perhaps these intimate links with the family provide the reason that visitors on a general tour make their acquaintance with portraits of its members in this room. It's always best to set up the cast of characters at the beginning of a story. A tour through the Mark Twain House truly follows the threads of an elaborate tale, in which Mark Twain is Mr. Samuel Clemens of Farmington Avenue. Visitors get to see him in his early forties, when he began to live in this house, and learn that his profuse hair and mustache were auburn and that he donned white suits only when relaxing in the summertime, like any Hartford gentleman. For business and social life, he wore the same dark suit everyone else wore, the garb he later said made men look like "a lot of crows." Then visitors see an image of the delicate but determined face of Livy, who brought the wealth into the family, supplied most of the funds for building the house, and ran it like a small, well-oiled business for all their Hartford years. And then there are the three girls. Well, it started with two, really—Jean, the baby, wasn't born until 1880, when they had lived in the house five and a half years.

Visitors are shown a portrait of Susy, a girl with a passionate temper like her father. She had a way with words like her father, too: "Once," her father wrote, "when she thought something very funny was going to happen (but it didn't) she was racked and torn with laughter, by anticipation. But apparently she still felt sure of her position, for she said, 'If it had happened I should have been transformed with glee.'" (She meant "transported," but she found the better word.) Susy wrote plays—one, *A Love Chase*, was performed in this very drawing room, and we have a picture of that to show, too, one of the rare images of family members in the house. When she was thirteen, she wrote a biography of her father, one of the best.

The drawing room was the place for formal hospitality, and after-dinner coffee for the ladies, and the place where the family and sometimes mystified guests gathered to hear Clemens play the piano and sing the African American spirituals he had learned from enslaved people when he was a boy in Missouri. The Paisley stenciling on the wall, the work of Associated Artists, reflects the Indian influence on the 1881 redecoration, an element of Victorian exoticism. THE MARK TWAIN HOUSE & MUSEUM. PHOTOGRAPHS BY JOHN GROO.

In 1889, the Clemens girls and their friends entertained Nook Farm neighbors in the drawing room with a play written by Susy, "a play along Greek lines," as Clemens referred to it, titled *A Love Chase*. From the left are Clara, Daisy Warner (daughter of George and Lilly), Jean, Susy, and friend Fannie Freese. THE MARK TWAIN HOUSE & MUSEUM COLLECTIONS.

The middle child, Clara, was born the very year they moved into the house. In her portrait as a child, you see the same strong, dark eyes that entranced Clemens when he viewed Livy's portrait on the *Quaker City*. The only daughter to reach old age, she was a living link to the Clemens era in the early days of the restoration of the house in the 1950s. She marked up a floor plan of the building, searching her memory in her eighties for the colors, objects, and designs that she had known in her childhood.

When she was little, she seemed to have a talent for injury. In a memoir, she described hurtling down the steep hillside behind the house on a toboggan and into an oak tree—an accident that bent one leg around "into the shape of a half moon" and nearly required amputation. "Once I was nearly drowned," she reported; "another time, when ill with croup, I was snatched from a blazing crib with my hair on fire; at the age of four I was discovered on the sixth story,

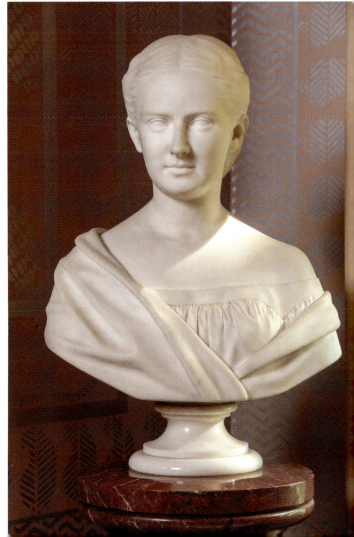

When Livy Clemens was a teenager, her parents commissioned a portrait bust from sculptor Samuel Conkey that now graces the drawing room. It was originally in the drawing room of the Langdon family home in Elmira, New York. A newspaper critic wrote of Conkey, an Elmira dentist who changed careers, "The charm of Mr. Conkey's work is, that he portrays an active, thinking mind in the joyous repose of an instant; and the appearance does not seem more fixed than it would in life."
THE MARK TWAIN HOUSE & MUSEUM, 1940.3.1. GIFT OF THE LANGDON FAMILY. PHOTOGRAPH BY JOHN GROO.

(Right) The three Clemens daughters were thoughtful and creative individuals. Susy (*near right*) inherited her father's incisive observation and wit. At thirteen, she wrote a biography of her father. Clara (*center*) showed a determination in her childhood that in later life led her to supervise her father's reputation with an iron hand. In the Hartford house, she and Susy were constant playmates. Jean (*far right*) was the baby of the family, born in 1880. She was deeply fond of animals, from the time when, as a toddler, she demanded that her father follow the cows on her aunt's farm, wherever they might roam, to her late-life activism with the Society for the Prevention of Cruelty to Animals. THE MARK TWAIN HOUSE & MUSEUM COLLECTIONS.

(Below) By the 1890s, even Jean (*center*) was approaching her teenage years. Clara (*right*) continued to be determined, explosive, and risk taking. Susy (*left*) was subdued, melancholy, and literary. Jean seemed to be happy whenever she could find animals to visit.
THE MARK TWAIN HOUSE & MUSEUM. GIFT OF OLIVIA LADA-MOCARSKI.

crawling around the inside of the banister of a hotel corridor, with a marble floor far below."

Clara survived all these accidents. Her father said, "I don't believe God cares much about meeting her," which may also have been the attitude of some of the editors of Mark Twain's papers when, in late life, she exercised her strong will in dictating which of her father's works should and should not be published. She admitted freely her inheritance of her mother's dogged persistence and her father's capacity for rage. She learned one morning when she was six that a favorite pet calf had been sold. (Continuing her accident streak, she had tried to ride it like a horse and was thrown off.) She said, "I raised such a hullabaloo that my screams reached even my father's study." The calf was quickly bought back again.

Finally, there's a picture of Jean, named for Samuel Clemens's mother. "Susie and Bay could not worship it more if it were a cat," Clemens wrote of Jean as a newborn ("Bay" was Clara's nickname). As a toddler, he said, she could be "sullen." Her eyes had the piercing quality of her father's, and she did not appear happy. Clemens wrote to his own mother, after whom she had been named, "Jean looks just like you, most of the time, & like me when the devil is in her." She was doted on during her Hartford childhood, which Clemens always thought of as an idyll. Her brief life, it will be seen, was not happy until she was close to the end of it.

The family firmly in mind, we pass between the drawn light curtains—*portières*—hanging in the wide opening between the drawing room and dining room. These were carefully created by a master seamstress from the photograph of Susy's play being performed in the room. In 1874, Potter led Mary Fairbanks into the dining room, too.

The Dining Room

The arrangement of library and dining-rooms are simply bewitching. Indeed adjectives begin to fail me. The rooms open into each other with folding doors. At the end of the dining-room is a fire-place with a window over the mantel commanding the same avenue view. On the side a broad window looking down upon the river and its pretty bank and meadow.

—Mary Mason Fairbanks, 1874

The window over the mantel still looks toward the avenue, and the window would look down on the North Branch of the Park River, were it still there. (The river was buried in an underground channel as a flood-control measure in the mid-twentieth century.) But the dining room table draws the eye, and this is where the guide gently warns visitors not to hold the back of a dining room chair to get a better look, which seems an irresistible impulse. The table is set in a seasonal arrangement devised by the curator: oysters at the start of a Christmas banquet, cake for Susy's fifteenth birthday party, and strawberries for a summer dessert party. The arrangements are often based on visitors' descriptions of what they ate here. Much of the china and silver on display belonged to the Langdons; knives, forks, and spoons are engraved with Livy's family name.

Around this table took place the family breakfasts Clara remembered nostalgically decades later—the Clemenses might enjoy broiled chicken, potatoes hashed with cream, coffee, and bread and butter—and the dinners with

The dining room as it appeared in 1896, while the Clemenses were in Europe. The elegant sideboard, with its inset decorative tile, was built to fit the niche in which it sits. The screen on the right masks the entrances to the kitchen hallway and the butler's pantry.
THE MARK TWAIN HOUSE & MUSEUM COLLECTIONS.

important and distinguished guests. These included Sir Henry Stanley, the journalist and speaker of the most famous formal greeting in history after he located the missionary David Livingston on the shores of Lake Tanganyika; actor Edwin Booth, who had overcome the family trauma of his brother's murder of Abraham Lincoln to become the most famous Hamlet of the Gilded

Age; General William T. Sherman, who had ravaged Georgia and was now ravaging the Western tribes; and Edward Bellamy, who envisioned a utopian socialist future that influenced some of the important figures of Franklin D. Roosevelt's New Deal half a century later. And one June night at dinner, an unreconstructed New Orleans writer, Grace King, passed from her annoyance at the self-righteous blather of a one-armed Union general to discuss the decor and the food:

> *An exquisite cut glass bowl in the centre filled with daisies, ferns, and grasses—a bunch of white roses was at each one's plate. . . . The candelabra were of twisted silver, with yellow candles and shades. Olives, salted almonds, and bonbons in curious dishes were on the table and decanters of quaint shape and color held the wine. The soup was "Claire"—the Clairest you ever saw, delicious flavor—sherry—Then fresh salmon, white wine sauce—Appolinaris [sic] water—sweet breads in cream served I vow, in what looked like pomatum pots—with covers (little flat round ones, exquisitely painted blue) claret, broiled chicken, green peas and new potatoes—(they are very rare here) tomato salad. I really cannot write a description of this—The salad dish is an immense deep plate of Hungarian ware. On the lettuce leaves were placed the tomatoes, sliced but still in shape—Over all was poured the Mayonnaise—and such instruments for serving—gold & silver—and carving. The dessert was a most magnificent dish—Charlotte Russe and wine jelly with candied cherries in it, with whipped cream—eaten of course with forks—and at last and prettiest of all—plates of strawberries with the stems still on—strawberries the size of walnuts, laid what I took for a form of whipped cream (a kind of rosette). It turned out to be powdered sugar—We of course dipped the strawberries in it and ate them with our fingers.*

Clara and Susy took in their parents' dinner parties from the staircase:

> *When dinner parties were given, Susy and I used to sit on the stairs and listen to the broken bits of conversation coming from the dining-room. We got into this habit because we used to hear so many peals of laughter in the distance that we would run to discover the cause of all the mirth. Almost always it turned out that Father was telling a funny story. Now, it happened that a few times Father had told the same story on various occasions when*

guests were dining at the house and we had calculated that each time the meal was about half over. So we used to announce to each other, "Father is telling the beggar story; they must have reached the meat course."

The entertainments were almost constant—"Indeed, my impression is that Father and Mother were constantly preparing for lunch parties or dinner parties," Clara recalled—and during the height of the season the family would spend as much as $100 a week for food (along with food-related incidentals, such as ice; for what this amount meant in twenty-first-century money, you can multiply by about 25 to get about $2,500). This was at a time when one of their housemaids made $150 a year along with room and board. The room's location where the Gilded Age home's lavish interior meets the plain painted walls of a hall leading to the kitchen provided an intersection of the Clemens family's lives and their servants' lives. As in many elegant dining rooms of the era, a screen hides the transition point between the support labor and the enjoyment of its fruits, the preparation of food and its serving. Griffin, despite his high status as the house's butler, would remain behind the screen until he was called on.

Here, too, visitors get a glimpse into the butler's pantry, Griffin's domain, notable for the curve of its outer wall, with glass-fronted cabinets carefully built to match the curve and yet allow space for five closely spaced windows. (Viewed from the outside, this show-off feature links the main part of the house to the kitchen wing on the first floor, the windows separated by variously patterned rectangles of multicolored brick.) The dark, elegant cabinetry, with hints of Clemens-owned or period porcelain and glass peeking through the cupboard windows, provides another visual high point. A small wooden sink was prescribed by Livy in 1874. Samuel reminded Potter of her wishes in a letter: "Mrs. Clemens says (so as to be sure it has not been forgotten) that she wants everything about the slab in the butler's pantry—to be of wood—the bowl, the slab, the back of the slab, & all—so there will be no excuse for dishes getting nicked."

Griffin shared, and sometimes dueled over, leadership of the kitchen area (to be visited later) with Catherine Leary, always known as "Katy." Leary was Livy's lady's maid but also "a potent influence, all over the premises," Clemens wrote. "Fidelity, truthfulness, courage, magnanimity, personal dignity, a pole-star for steadiness—these were her equipment, along with a good store of Irish warmth."

The dining room was the scene of lavish dinner parties during the Clemenses' tenure. The original sideboard, returned to its niche in the wall, found its way back to the house by loan and finally by purchase. The window directly over the fireplace was a feature often remarked on by visitors during the Clemens period. THE MARK TWAIN HOUSE & MUSEUM. PHOTOGRAPH BY JOHN GROO.

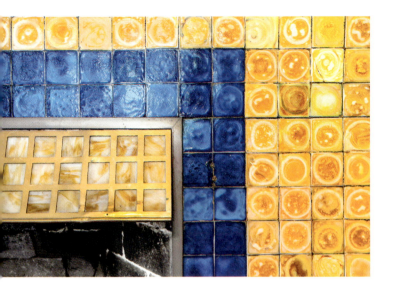

During the redecoration of the house in 1881, the new fireplace and overmantel featured Tiffany opalescent glass tiles that filled the fireplace surround. The smoke shield (*lower left*) featured translucent onyx tiles. A similar fireplace treatment by the famed designer survives in the Park Avenue Armory in New York.
THE MARK TWAIN HOUSE & MUSEUM. PHOTOGRAPH BY ALANA BORGES GORDON.

Livy Clemens hired Leary after summering in Elmira in 1880; Leary's sister had done similar work for Livy's brother's family there. Over the next thirty years, Leary worked for the family. In later life she ran a small boarding house in New York City while living on a $10,000 bequest from Twain and a monthly pension from Clara. In 1922, she returned to Elmira and lived the remainder of her years in the home she inherited from her parents. Her 1925 memoir, *A Lifetime with Mark Twain*, provides valuable insight to the lives of the Clemens family and is rich with anecdotes and detail about life in the Hartford house.

But let us return to the dining room and kitchen, where Leary and Griffin had a rivalry going that mirrored the world outside, in which Irish immigrants vied with African Americans for service jobs. When they argued about who worked the hardest, Clara reported, Clemens squelched them: "You are both too clever to do much work."

At times, during dinners with guests, Griffin, behind the screen, could be heard laughing at Samuel's stories during dinner, sometimes before the punch line (he had heard most of them before). Leary recalled dessert, "no, never plain ordinary ice cream—we always had our ice cream put up in some wonderful shapes—like flowers or cherubs, little angels—all different kinds and different shapes and colors—oh, everything lovely!" And she described how at the end of the meal, the ladies would withdraw to the drawing room for coffee while the men would "sit (lounge, I think they call it) around the table and have a little more champagne (maybe)."

The side of the room toward the river is dominated by a high, wide Eastlake-style sideboard, clearly made to fit the niche in the wall in which it sits, with huge, decorative, medieval-style hinges, and decorated with both classical and Japanese tiles. The two Japanese tiles are decorated with cranes, a common

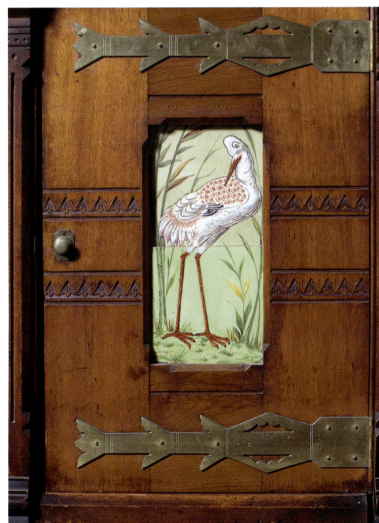

In the eclectic style so favored by the Victorians, tiles with classical scenes contrast with the Japanese tiles in a way they found charming and later generations found clashing. A Japanese tile in one of the doors in the sideboard displays a traditional crane design.

THE MARK TWAIN HOUSE & MUSEUM. PHOTOGRAPHS BY JOHN GROO.

At the head of the dinner table, Samuel Clemens held forth with stories both funny and incisive, sometimes rising from his chair to pace back and forth for emphasis. But he also listened—to journalist Henry Stanley's tales of African exploration, to writer Grace King's descriptions of Creole New Orleans, and to neighbor Harriet Beecher Stowe's stories of the old antislavery days.
THE MARK TWAIN HOUSE & MUSEUM. PHOTOGRAPH BY JOHN GROO.

motif. The Elmira home of Livy's sister, Susan Crane, where the family spent summers, contains fireplace tiles also showing cranes, traditionally thought to have been a visual pun on the family name. When the sideboard was ordered for this space, possibly in Boston in 1876, that thought may have been in the Clemenses' minds. A contemporary photograph of the dining room shows the sideboard being used not only as a locked cabinet for silver but also as a place to display a variety of ornate teapots and pitchers. The display case of cut glass across the table from this was described by King in 1887; it's in fact a piano with the strings removed.

Because of the room's transitional status between the family's world and the servants' world, it is also the location of Livy's work desk, from which she managed the bustling workplace for the servants, planning out meals, gatherings, and events day after day. To keep up with this intense level of management, she kept a box of candies, made by the New York chocolatier Huyler's, in a drawer, a family friend remembered years later. Sometimes, as she confided to her mother in an 1879 letter, it was all too much: "In this day women must be everything. They must keep up with all the current literature, they must know all about art, they must help in one or two benevolent societies—they must be perfect mothers—they must be perfect housekeepers & graceful gracious hostesses . . . above all they must make their houses 'charming' & so on without end."

The Library

At the rear of the Library is a Conservatory opposite the fire-place of the dining-room. Imagine the winter attractions of these rooms, while the summer charms are not less apparent. A generous bay window in the side of the library lets in a whole sweep of rich landscape and a fire-place on the opposite side is surmounted by a quaint oaken mantel of ancient English carving.

—MARY MASON FAIRBANKS, 1874

The library, with its dark depths ending in a conservatory—a glass-enclosed bright wonderland of tropical plants—is a main attraction for visitors. It had many functions, from entertainment center (yes, the words in those brown rectangular things on the shelves provided deeply visual and sonorous entertainment long before the days of flickering screens—adventure, poetry, love stories, travel, and the whole range of human experience) to storyland to stage for the family production of *The Prince and the Pauper* to a locale for almost constant games of charades. It was, too, the locale for cigars and brandy and serious discussion of the politics of the day. It could also serve as a place for a late supper after the tiring day of travel, as Clara related: "Sometimes, on evenings when Father and Mother returned from New York and the weather was bitterly cold, George served supper for them on a small table in front of the fire in the library."

   The library is also a reminder that, aside from being a showplace of decoration and style, and the place where a loving and idiosyncratic family lived (and a difficult range of housekeeping was undertaken), this house was a workplace for Samuel Clemens. In various studies around the house and grounds, and in their summer retreats in Elmira, he was in a constant state of notetaking, writing, editing, discarding, and rewriting. "You need not expect to get your book right the first time," he wrote to his brother Orion, who was working on a memoir. "Go to work and revamp or rewrite it. God only exhibits his thunder and

The library was the social center of the house after dinner (or indeed at any time of day). The great chimneypiece from Ayton Castle in Scotland dominates the space. The room provided a place to have a quick supper on returning from a trip, or to entertain friends, or to tell stories to the children. These stories were often dependent on items on the mantel and had to follow a progression from a painting of a cat in an Elizabethan ruff collar to the right of the chimneypiece to a painting of a woman the children named "Emmeline" on the left.
THE MARK TWAIN HOUSE & MUSEUM. PHOTOGRAPH BY JOHN GROO.

Olivia Clemens's mother, Olivia Lewis Langdon, sits in her favorite rocking chair next to the fireplace in the library. Mrs. Langdon's yearly visits of several months were an important part of the family's life in more ways than one—she was a major financial benefactor of the family. THE MARK TWAIN HOUSE & MUSEUM COLLECTIONS.

lightning at intervals, and so they always command attention." While Clemens lived in the Hartford house, he created his best-known works—*The Adventures of Tom Sawyer*, *Adventures of Huckleberry Finn*, *The Prince and the Pauper*, and *A Connecticut Yankee in King Arthur's Court*. And there were dozens of short works—lectures, after-dinner speeches, and magazine pieces written during those seventeen years. These required the work of a first editor—Livy— and that critique was a controversial one. In the 1920s, it occasioned a serious feud between two literary critics: Van Wyck Brooks, who thought that Livy and the comforts of Hartford life had "sivilized" Mark Twain and restrained him from becoming a great writer, and Bernard DeVoto, who sprang to the author's defense. Here, in this library, is where much of this controversial editing took place, so this wonderful room with its burbling fountain and massive chimney-piece deserves a place in literary history for many reasons.

At the south end of the library, the glass conservatory provides a focal point of light and green, with a gently burbling fountain adding a calming element to the room. The settee provided a place to lie back and read the volumes of history, travel, and fantasy that enriched the family members' lives.
THE MARK TWAIN HOUSE & MUSEUM. PHOTOGRAPH BY JOHN GROO.

Visitor Thomas Russell was sixteen when he took this photograph of the library and conservatory in 1896. The statue of Eve was sculpted by Karl Gerhardt, a German American sculptor from Hartford who was a protégé of the Clemenses. THE MARK TWAIN HOUSE & MUSEUM. GIFT OF THOMAS RUSSELL.

Here's the process as described by Susy, who, with Clara, was allowed to listen in on these sessions—making them the only two children who ever had the truly uncensored *Huckleberry Finn* read to them by a parent:

> *Ever since papa and mama were married papa has written his books and then taken them to mama in manuscript and she has expergated [sic] them. Papa read Huckleberry Finn to us in manuscript, just before it came out, and then he would leave parts of it with mama to expergate, while he went off to the study to work, and sometimes Clara and I would be sitting with mama while she was looking the manuscript over, and I remember so well, with what pangs of regret we used to see her turn down the leaves of the pages, which meant some delightfully terrible part must be scratched out.*

Another reason for the literary importance of this room is that it was where Clemens performed, as it were, five-finger exercises for his writing and lectures. This was again under the supervision of his daughters, who required him to make stories out of thin air, using objects in the room as visual guides. These included pictures and bric-a-brac on the mantel; the story, the girls said, had to begin with a painting of a cat in an Elizabethan ruffed collar and then move to the next item on the mantel, then to the next, then to the next, with the end piece an Impressionist painting of a lady in blue, whom Clemens and the children dubbed "Emmeline."

"Those bric-a-bracs were never allowed a peaceful day, a reposeful day, a restful Sabbath," Clemens wrote. "In their lives there was no Sabbath; in their lives there was no peace; they knew no existence but a monotonous career of violence and bloodshed. In the course of time the bric-a-brac and the pictures showed wear."

Clara reported a similar storytelling game involving the paintings on the walls. "Passing from picture to picture, his power of invention led us into countries and among human figures that held us spellbound. He treated a Medusa head according to his own individual method, the snakes being sometimes changed to laurel leaves that tickled joy in Medusa's hair and inspired thoughts of victory." These stories were required by the "insatiable desires of his tiny auditors," she said.

The great carved oak chimneypiece that Mary Fairbanks saw on her tour with Edward Tuckerman Potter in April 1874 was purchased in Edinburgh during the Clemenses' trip the year before and shipped to Hartford. It was not so ancient as Fairbanks thought: Ayton Castle, its source, was not a very old castle, having been built in 1851 as part of the same fascination with things medieval that brought the Gothic craze to America. The mantel is carved with masks, scrolls, musical instruments, and garlands of fruit, along with a coat of arms that combines the heraldry of the two families of *nouveaux riches* who owned the castle, the Mitchells and the Ineses. It also contains the mottoes of the two families: "Je reçois pour donner" and "Deo Favente" ("I receive in order to give" in Old French, and "with God's favor" in Latin). Under these the Clemenses placed a pierced brass plate with another motto, plucked from Ralph Waldo Emerson, more suited to the bustling hospitality of their home: "The ornament of a house is the friends who frequent it." (The "is the friends" in this motto, chosen by Livy, grated on Mark's fine literary ear. He wrote to a friend, "I do not mean that the grammar is not correct, I merely mean that in one place it all at once arrests the flow of your serenity for a moment, like gravel in the bread.")

At the end of the library, the eye and ear keep returning to the gently burbling fountain in the conservatory. In his novel *A Little Journey in the World*, the Clemenses' neighbor Charles Dudley Warner (the newspaper editor and collaborator on *The Gilded Age*) re-created the Nook Farm scene, calling Hartford "Brandon," and described a conservatory much like this:

> *A spacious place with a fountain and cool vines and flowering plants, not a tropical hothouse in a stifling atmosphere, in which nothing could live except orchids and flowers born near the Equator, but a garden with a temperature adapted to human lungs, where one could sit and enjoy the sunshine, and the odor of flowers, and the clear and not too incessant notes of Mexican birds.*

It was not, however, a bird of any nationality but a snake that Clara described emerging from the conservatory one day as she and Susy sat on their father's lap: "Father dropped us both to the floor and seizing a pair of tongs from the fireplace lifted the snake in the air and precipitated him through a door in the bay window that faced the wooded ravine." Keeping a keen eye out for reptiles, the volunteers of the University of Connecticut's Master Gardeners program today are carefully nurturing and restoring the magnificence of the conservatory.

The conservatory brought the summer into the winter for the family and provided a backdrop for games described by Clemens in which he got down on his hands and knees and played the role of an elephant for his daughters. The existing vine, a ficus, climbing up the glass is believed to be descended from a plant the Clemenses owned. THE MARK TWAIN HOUSE & MUSEUM. PHOTOGRAPH BY JOHN GROO.

The Mahogany Room

Opening from the Library is a suite of rooms whose tasteful appointments and dainty boudoir indicate their presiding genius.

—Mary Mason Fairbanks, 1874

Mary Fairbanks presumably meant Livy as the "presiding genius" of the house. Livy not only paid the bills for building the house and planned its eastern orientation but also laid out the rooms for Potter. This suite—a large bedroom with windows looking out at the level of the porch, with a dressing room and bathroom attached—was called the mahogany room, after the mahogany bedroom set built for it and some of the woodwork. It was used for prominent guests.

"He used to give me a royal chamber on the ground floor," recalled Clemens's close friend, the novelist and editor William Dean Howells. Clemens, he said, would

> *come in at night after I had gone to bed to turn off the burglar alarm so that the family should not be roused if anyone tried to get in at my window. This would be after we had sat up late, he smoking the last of his innumerable cigars, and soothing his tense nerves with a mild hot Scotch, while we both talked and talked and talked, of everything in the heavens and the earth, and the waters under the earth.*

Yes, Clemens had a burglar alarm on the windows. The alarms were the only electric items in the house, operating on dry-cell batteries. In her biography of her father, begun when she was thirteen years old, daughter Susy reported on this device:

> *He has the mind of an author exactly, some of the simplest things he cant understand. Our burglar-alarm is often out of order, and papa had been obliged to take the mahogany-room off from the alarm altogether for a time, because the burglar-alarm had been in the habit of ringing even when the mahogany-room was closed.*

When Grace King stayed in these rooms in October 1887, she was lost in the charm of this elegant little suite, so accessible to the library, which was a treasure trove for an author of regional tales full of wit and insight. King wrote her mother from the mahogany room:

> *I certainly cannot go to sleep to night without giving you a little account of my gorgeous surroundings. You must know that I am at the Clemens; came over for dinner to day. I have a large bedroom, a large dressing room, & a bath room with every accomplishment in the way of water and bath. The maid has hung up my dresses and placed all my things for the night on the dressing tables. There are lights lighted everywhere, and I do feel very much like Beauty did when the Beast left her alone in the palace.*

When there were no guests, the room did not go untenanted. It was the dressing room for the theatricals the Clemenses put on in the library, where the conservatory formed a natural stage. A costume for a prince of the Middle Ages lies on the bed, representing the garb daughter Susy wore when she played Edward Tudor, Prince of Wales, in a theatrical performance of her father's *The Prince and the Pauper*. And it was here that Livy wrapped gifts at Christmas and prepared baskets to be distributed to the city's poor. "Mrs. Clemens would be fixing baskets in the room off the Library (they always used to do the Christmas things there) and she used to do up about fifty baskets herself," recalled Katy Leary. Clara remembered:

> *Mother had almost a German talent for thoroughness in any task she undertook. . . . If she could not be found anywhere in the house, one might guess that she was busy in the "mahogany room," writing lists of names and trying to determine the needs or wishes of each individual.*

The room is dominated by the bed and bureau, the recovered remnants of a four-piece set sold at auction after the Clemens family left the house. (The whereabouts of a side table of the same design and a mahogany rocking chair are unknown.) The Clemenses ordered the set built in 1875, and the acquisition made the news: the Springfield *Daily Republican* of June 18 reported that "Mark Twain, to have the furniture of his house correspond with its other peculiarities, has ordered an unique chamber-set, made of mahogany with diamond-shaped panels of blue and white china plentifully bespangling it, with heavy blue satin draperies, the whole, of only three pieces, to cost $600."

In a room reserved for guests, the mahogany bed—part of what a newspaper called "an unique chamber-set, made of mahogany with diamond-shaped panels of blue and white china plentifully bespangling it"—was sold in 1903 but has since returned to the Clemens home. THE MARK TWAIN HOUSE & MUSEUM. PHOTOGRAPH BY JOHN GROO.

Another piece of the "unique chamber-set" is the mirrored bureau next to the door to the library. Access to the Clemenses' extensive collection of books was an added benefit to a stay with the family for literary figures such as Grace King and William Dean Howells. THE MARK TWAIN HOUSE & MUSEUM. PHOTOGRAPH BY JOHN GROO.

During the mahogany room suite's 2015–2016 restoration, the decision was made to use a wallpaper designed by Candace Wheeler, who was part of the Associated Artists group with Louis Tiffany and others who redecorated the Clemens house in 1881. Her dramatic "Honeycomb" wallpaper (*left*) covered the walls; the "Spiderweb" pattern (*center*), also featuring honeybees, covers the ceiling; and the dado (*right*)—the section of paper nearest the floor—features "skeps," old-style beehives made of straw.

THE MARK TWAIN HOUSE & MUSEUM. PHOTOGRAPHS BY JOHN GROO.

The suite underwent a major restoration in 2015–2016. With earlier wallpaper restoration rejected, and no apparent clue remaining as to the original wallpaper, the museum decided to honor one of the original designers, Candace Wheeler. Her "Honeycomb" wallpaper now graces the walls of the room, and a "Spiderweb" pattern on the ceiling adds to its dazzling splendor. The bedroom set was taken out of storage, awaiting its blue-satin draperies as the windows awaited their drapes when budgets would allow for it. Reproduction cut-pile carpets now cover the floor, and, as a crowning touch, a curator located a print of Rembrandt's *The Night Watch* similar to one the Clemenses purchased in The Hague in 1879. "The etching was very expensive, twenty dollars," Livy wrote, "but I decided if Mr. Clemens liked it that we would get it . . . Mr. Clemens went to see it and liked it, so we possess the etching."

A small dressing room with a fireplace surrounded by blue and red tiles looks out at the level of the porch. A gas heater in the fireplace made it the warmest place in the house to study, Clara Clemens remembered. Finally, there is the bathroom, its post-Clemens tub replaced with a zinc-lined one in a wooden frame more appropriate to the period. A mahogany toilet is adorned with a book of nineteenth-century toilet paper made at Congress Mills in Windsor Locks, Connecticut. On the shelf above the sink stands a box of cherry-flavored toothpaste, a container of nineteenth-century dental floss, a straight razor, and bay rum aftershave.

In its present appearance, the mahogany room has been returned to the condition William Dean Howells and Grace King found it in: a royal chamber, a castle fit for both Beauty and the Beast.

The dressing room (*top*) and the bathroom made the mahogany room more a suite than a room, though the family always used the "room" designation. The dressing room featured a tile-lined hearth featuring a gas heater, where daughter Clara Clemens studied on winter evenings. The bathroom, in a recent restoration, acquired a tinned copper tub and water closet, along with appropriate porcelain sinks. THE MARK TWAIN HOUSE & MUSEUM. PHOTOGRAPHS BY JOHN GROO.

THE SECOND FLOOR

Up the broad, easy staircase, which seems, somehow, not to encroach upon the spacious hall, we follow our friend Mr. Potter, who peoples and embellishes the second floor for us.

—Mary Mason Fairbanks, 1874

The *Cleveland Journal* correspondent and the architect alighted on a landing, which, like so many places in this house, was designed for seating and relaxation around a fireplace. Today's visitor sees a marble bust of the Reverend Henry Ward Beecher, a larger-than-life man—as mentioned, one of the many Beecher connections who intersected with both Samuel's and Livy's lives, but a particular object of admiration for Clemens. Beecher, so famous as a preacher that thousands came to his Brooklyn church weekly, was felled by an adultery scandal that shook and split Nook Farm. Clemens remained steadfastly behind Beecher. He wrote, "What a pity—that so insignificant a matter as the chastity or unchastity of Elizabeth Tilton could clip the locks of this Samson."

Beecher looks like Samson in the bust, if a jowly one. After a visit to Clemens, a *New York World* reporter wrote that the bust "had been done by a young man whom he and his wife had sent to Rome to be educated as a sculptor." (The sculptor was Gerhardt, who did the bust of Clemens in the entry hall and other works in the house; the city, in fact, was Paris.) "Then," the reporter quoted Clemens as saying, "we are well rewarded by this bust, which is the best one ever done of the great American preacher."

A long, well-lighted room to the right of the staircase served as Livy's private sitting room. After Jean's birth in 1880, it was taken over by Susy as her room, and that is the way it is portrayed today, down to the photos propped on the dresser mirror and the seaweed collected on shoreline excursions. Years later, when they were selling the house, Livy asked particularly that Susy's seaweed and shells be carefully preserved, because by then these pieces of memorabilia—along with all memories of this bright and brilliant daughter—carried a special and tragic significance.

From the second floor, the great staircase sweeps upward toward the clerestory windows. It is a nod to Potter's skills as an architect of churches and a source of light in a house that could be dark. THE MARK TWAIN HOUSE & MUSEUM. PHOTOGRAPH BY JOHN GROO.

(Opposite page) A bust of the Reverend Henry Ward Beecher, an abolitionist icon and innovative, wildly popular preacher, dominates the second-floor landing. An adultery scandal involving the minister split the Nook Farm intelligentsia; the Clemenses were on Beecher's side. HARRIET BEECHER STOWE CENTER. PHOTOGRAPH BY JOHN GROO.

The second-floor landing was a living space in itself, with its own fireplace and furniture, including a settee bench. The living quarters of the house were located on this floor. The wall stenciling added by Associated Artists in 1881 provided a brightening element. THE MARK TWAIN HOUSE & MUSEUM. PHOTOGRAPH BY JOHN GROO.

At the threshold of the Clemenses' bedroom, an inviting alcove offers a place to read or sew on a rainy day. It's one of the many nooks and crannies that a later resident said made the house "a world unto itself." THE MARK TWAIN HOUSE & MUSEUM. PHOTOGRAPH BY JOHN GROO.

A room off the alcove served as Livy's own place to sew, read, and write letters, until Susy became old enough to leave the adjacent nursery. Then she settled in with her teenage treasures, including the dried seaweed on her bureau, that Livy remembered to have packed up and carefully treasured years later when the family left the house. THE MARK TWAIN HOUSE & MUSEUM. PHOTOGRAPH BY JOHN GROO.

Samuel and Livy's Bedroom

Ahead of Potter and Fairbanks was the entrance to Samuel and Livy's room, which Fairbanks left undescribed, but we can people and embellish it ourselves. At the time of Fairbanks's visit, the great walnut bed that serves as centerpiece in the room may have been sitting in the shop in Venice where the Clemenses would find it four and a half years later and buy it for the equivalent of $200. (Again, multiply by 25 for today's rough value, $5,000.) The bed immediately draws the eye, and Clemens was aware of this quality: in late life, he would have himself photographed and interviewed in it, his wild hair and Satanic expression contrasting with the gamboling carved angels, the darkness of the wood contrasting with his white nightshirt.

But when the bed was brought into the house in 1879, it became the occasion for Clemens stories, particularly one in which the author realized he had been swearing in the adjacent bathroom within Livy's hearing. He had tried to make his way out of the room to avoid her but was defeated by the Clemenses' practice of putting their pillows at the foot of the bed rather than the head. "You know how it is when you are convinced that somebody behind you is looking steadily at you. You have to turn your face—you can't help it." He turned: "Against the white pillows I saw the black head—I saw the young and beautiful face; and I saw the gracious eyes with a something in them which I had never seen there before. They were snapping and flashing with indignation."

The bed that Sam and Livy Clemens bought in Venice in 1879 accompanied Sam to his various abodes after Livy's death in 1904. In 1906, as a world celebrity, he decided to have a series of publicity photos taken in bed. They show him reading, smoking, and writing surrounded by the angels adorning his bedposts. THE MARK TWAIN HOUSE & MUSEUM. GIFT OF EULABEE DIX.

The great bed, bought in Venice in 1879, dominates the Clemens bedroom. The stories around it are legion. A portrait of a robin on the wall is reputed to have been done by all three daughters, as the signature "JSC" includes the first-name initials of Jean, Susy, and Clara. The portrait over the mantel is of Heidelberg Castle in Germany, which figures in Clemens's *A Tramp Abroad*.
THE MARK TWAIN HOUSE & MUSEUM. PHOTOGRAPH BY JOHN GROO.

The bed was arranged with the pillows at the foot, possibly for comfort, but, Clemens said, perhaps also for a view of the angels on the headboard who gave "peace to the sleepers." The angels on each corner of the bed, easily removable, became playthings for the daughters of the Clemens family. THE MARK TWAIN HOUSE & MUSEUM. PHOTOGRAPHS BY JOHN GROO.

The pillows at the foot of the bed rather than at the headboard provide the subject of a quick guessing game for visitors today—can you see what's different about this bed? But the reason for the placement of the pillows seems to have a double-barreled Twainian explanation: It had "carved angels enough surmounting its twisted columns and its headboard and footboard to bring peace to the sleepers, and pleasant dreams," Clemens wrote. The other explanation raises a chuckle and may be folklore, as the source is hard to trace: "He wanted to see what he had paid for."

Recuperating from the toboggan accident that injured her leg so badly, Clara got to stay here:

> *During this period I slept in my parents' bedroom in a large Dutch bed that had an angel on each of the four posts.*

Since earliest infancy my sisters and I had always adored this bed. The angels could be removed and we frequently took them down and washed them in a small bathtub.

The bed and other large items of carved furniture are set against a bluish-green wallpaper; the color was recalled in old age by Clara when she sketched in the furnishings she remembered on a plan of the house's rooms. The paper displays a pattern of small blooms and leaves in repeated groupings, against a subtle crosshatched background, reflecting Britain's Japanese-influenced Aesthetic School. Over the mantel is a romantic print, a view of a ruined section of Heidelberg Castle high above the Neckar River in Germany. The Clemenses visited there on the same 1878–1879 European trip during which they bought the bed, and Clemens and his Hartford friend Reverend Twichell rowed down the river for a while.

There's another literary connection here. In his reconstruction of this pleasant day in the travel book that grew out of this trip, *A Tramp Abroad*, a mixture of fact and fantasy, Clemens put the two of them on a raft instead of a rowboat—and had the raft strike the Heidelberg bridge and go "all to smash and scatteration." He had rafts much on his mind. While in Europe to work on this new travel book, an attempt to build on the success of *The Innocents Abroad*,

"A DEEP AND TRANQUIL ECSTASY."

The lithograph of Heidelberg Castle over the mantel in the bedroom also shows the bridge over the Neckar River. In an illustration for *A Tramp Abroad*, Clemens and his friend Joseph Twichell (called "Harris" in the book) ride a raft down the river, innocently enjoying the scene as they head toward the raft's demolition in a crash against that bridge. The incident was a fantasy based on a real trip and has more of *Huckleberry Finn* than Heidelberg in it. THE MARK TWAIN HOUSE & MUSEUM COLLECTIONS.

he was in the midst of a three-year gap in his writing of a very different book he had begun in 1876—a "boy's book" that was to be a sequel to *Tom Sawyer*. He had left his protagonists, Huckleberry Finn and the enslaved but escaping Jim, drenched just before he left off at the end of chapter 16. They had smashed their own raft in a collision with a steamboat. He had then placed the manuscript on one of the pigeonhole shelves in his study, where it waited quietly for him to regain inspiration—or, rather, while modern American literature awaited its birth, if you go by Ernest Hemingway, who said that "all modern American literature comes from one book by Mark Twain called *Huckleberry Finn*."

There are signs of family in the room—photographic portraits of the children, along with Jane Lampton Clemens and Jervis and Olivia Lewis Langdon. There is also a crude watercolor of a robin signed "JSC"—an item that by repute was the creation of all three daughters, their given-name initials making up the signature. Or perhaps the "C" is for Clemens, and the robin was just a rainy afternoon project for Susy and her small sister Jean.

Grandmamma's Room

Here are guest rooms, opening upon balconies that command landscapes to inspire a poet or an artist.

—Mary Mason Fairbanks, 1874

"Ma's bedroom" is what Clemens called this chamber in a letter to his brother Orion several months after Fairbanks's visit, when the family finally moved into the house but had to live on the second floor, as the building was "full of carpenters yet." "This your room at Livy's," a family friend called it in a letter to Olivia Lewis Langdon when he had the privilege of staying in it as a guest. It had indeed been designed specifically as a place for Livy's widowed mother to spend several months a year with the family. She, in fact, is seen in a photograph in the library, sitting

Olivia Lewis Langdon's grandchildren recalled her generosity in distributing gifts to all the children of the family at her home in Elmira when it was her own birthday. A widow, "she was mistress in her own house," read her obituary in 1890.
THE MARK TWAIN & MUSEUM COLLECTIONS.

A writing desk that belonged to the Langdons is displayed in Mrs. Langdon's room. Over the writing area are carved gryphons. The ceiling stencil in the Langdon bedroom was reproduced from traces of the original stenciling found on the back of a canvas covering applied to the ceiling.
THE MARK TWAIN HOUSE & MUSEUM. PHOTOGRAPHS BY JOHN GROO.

in a small rocker next to the fireplace in a silk dress and bonnet, a book in her lap and a quiet smile on her face.

Her visits of several months were happily anticipated: "Now, Mother dear," Samuel wrote one October, "we shall be ready for you any day this week, & the sooner the satisfactorier. Livy has got a new boiler in & it's a great-geyser-of-a-Yellowstone for liberality in the way of hot water." Her departures were regretted, as Livy wrote three months later: "Susy said tonight 'The fire has gone out in Grandmamma's room.' And we all feel how lonely it is."

Langdon shared her husband's abolitionist stance and his deep faith in Thomas K. Beecher's creedless Congregationalism. Like her daughter Livy, "she was intellectual and she was practical," a granddaughter, Ida Langdon, wrote in 1955. "She was socially inclined and socially gifted. She was interested in the furnishing of [her] house, in the collecting of a 'family library,' the cultivation and distribution of her hot-house flowers and fruits." She presided over social gatherings that were "warmly hospitable occasions, marked by considerable originality—probably Victorian of the pleasantest type." And, like Livy, she was tough. "She was mistress in her own house," read her obituary. "Her men and maids fell into their places without question or resistance, and yet without any sense of tyranny or oppression."

Olivia Langdon had in fact checked with Mary Fairbanks before approving Clemens as a prospective husband for her daughter. She had heard that he had reformed from past conduct and asked sharply, "From what standard of

"Your room at Livy's," a friend called Mrs. Langdon's guest room on the second floor. Livy's mother was a frequent and long-term guest. THE MARK TWAIN HOUSE & MUSEUM. PHOTOGRAPH BY JOHN GROO.

conduct, from what habitual life, did this change, or improvement, or reformation commence?" She was a major beneficiary after Jervis Langdon died in 1870, leaving a million dollars to his heirs, and in the early days of the Clemenses' residence in the house she continued to help Livy with furnishing it.

Livy wrote her from Venice in 1878, "I have done a good deal of shopping, how I should like to talk over all the things with you—When we get the things home you will see how many of them you have given us." She followed up in another letter: "Oh Mother you are too good to send us so much money. It is too much—you are too good to us." And later: "I think you are the very best Mother in the world, how could you offer that thousand dollars!" Olivia's generosity persisted even after Clemens's fame brought him his own earned prosperity. Shortly before her death in 1890, she loaned Clemens $10,000 to help pay for work on a mechanical typesetter he had invested in—an investment that, in fact, was gradually bringing the family to financial ruin.

The bedroom set in the room reflects an odd turnabout—they are indeed the furnishings of a guest room of the period, but not this one. They come from

Olivia Langdon's house in Elmira, so it's possible that during visits there the Clemenses themselves were guests in this bed. Katharine Seymour Day, the grandniece of Harriet Beecher Stowe and the woman to whom we can be grateful that the house in Hartford was saved at all, rushed to Elmira and bought the set in 1939 as the Langdon house was about to go under the wrecker's ball.

The Nursery

Here is the nursery with its gay hangings, it[s] bright carpet, its fantastic, story telling tiles beside the fire place. Here are windows that take in a flood of early sunshine and perfume of the violets that grow on the bank beneath—and music of the robins—the cheeriest room in the house for a child to thrive and delight in. This door opens into the mother's little parlor—that into the father's study.

—Mary Mason Fairbanks, 1874

A new governess arrives: "A snug small room; a round table by a cheerful fire; an arm-chair high-backed and old-fashioned.... A more reassuring introduction for a new governess could scarcely be conceived; there was no grandeur to overwhelm, no stateliness to embarrass." This governess is not the Clemenses' Rosina Hay—in fact, it's the heroine of Charlotte Brontë's *Jane Eyre*, arriving at Mr. Rochester's home, in a book we know the Clemens girls loved.

But it could very well have been Rosina Hay arriving at the Clemenses' rented home in January 1874. Livy wrote to Mollie Clemens, Orion's wife, "I have found a little German maid who is entirely accustomed to children and comes highly

Rosina Hay, a German American from Hartford, was the constant companion of Susy and Clara Clemens, and then of Jean, from before the family moved into the Hartford house until 1883. Here she sits in the grounds holding the toddler Susy and infant Clara in 1875. COURTESY OF KEVIN MAC DONNELL, AUSTIN, TEXAS.

recommended. She was taking care of children in Fenwick when we were there." The nursery was Hay's domain—in photos her eyes sparkle, her mouth is serious, her forehead is slightly bowed. She is usually shown holding the toddler Susy and the baby Clara.

Hay was German American, the sister of a Hartford barber, and Livy called her "a quiet lady like German girl." Clemens added that she was "very lively, and active, and spirited, with a strong sense of humor, and she had a rollicking laugh that came easily and was as catching as the smallpox." Livy wrote Samuel from Elmira shortly after they hired her to say, "Don't forget to have Rossa's [sic] brother to shave you if you have time so you may tell him how well she does." She was present during many childhood dramas. In one, she and a wet nurse hired for Clara took the little girls for a stroll, and someone pushed the canopy of Clara's baby carriage forward. The metal supporting arm "caught the baby's middle finger, nipping the end of it nearly off." The coachman, Patrick McAleer, bound the wound in tobacco to stanch the blood until the doctor arrived.

This was the accident-prone Clara, of course, but some suspicion fell on Susy, who was known as "the Modoc" (after a West Coast Native American tribe) for her wild ways. "From early babyhood until she was three and a half years old, she was addicted to sudden & raging tempests of passion," Clemens reported. "Coaxing was tried; reasoning was tried; diversion was tried; even bribery. . . . At last we dropped every feature of the system utterly & resorted to flogging." The parents were the ones who administered corporal punishment, which Clemens said worked like a charm; Clara, years later, remembered her and Susy's fear of their mother's physical punishments. In the Victorian worldview, this was a form of love, though it makes us shudder today.

Clemens describes Hay as "a good disciplinarian, & faithful to her orders. She was not allowed to talk to the children in any tongue but German." At one point, five-year-old Clara, tired of this practice, exclaimed, "I wish God had made Rosa in English." Hay also had gentler roles: She wrote the girls' letters to Santa Claus for them and on Susy's third birthday presented her with a "pink azalia [sic] in lavish bloom," Livy reported. From Clemens's later description, the children's lives were idyllic, and, certainly, hindsight set a glow on the era. But there was plenty of drama. Clemens described the fire Clara later spoke of in her memoirs: "A croup-kettle set fire to Bay's crib & canopy, & Rosa snatched Bay from the midst of the flames, just in time to save her life. Then Rosa & I threw the burning bedding out of the window—though it looked, for awhile, as if the house must go."

In 1968, members of the Mark Twain Memorial carefully removed a piece of the mantel in the room that had been the Clemens children's nursery but now served as an office. Behind it they found a scrap of wallpaper showing frogs, mice, and cats. The paper turned out to be of the Clemens era and was found to be a design by the famed children's book illustrator Walter Crane.
THE MARK TWAIN HOUSE & MUSEUM COLLECTIONS.

The two brass beds in the room are derived from Clara's memory as expressed on the floor plan that she annotated in the 1950s. The way the room is portrayed today represents its arrangement after the birth of Jean in 1880. One brass bed is for Clara, six years old when Jean was born, and the other is for Hay, on call twenty-four hours a day. The crib—an original Clemens family possession—is for Jean. Susy, the teenager, moved into the adjacent room through the door that Fairbanks referred to as the entry to "the mother's little parlor." The toys in the room were not owned by the girls but were typical of the period. One toy does have a link to the Clemenses: a doll dressed in a fashionable gray coat and beret of the 1870s, her gloves placed decorously on her lap, belonged to a cousin, Ida Langdon, who often played with the Clemens girls.

The wallpaper, with its delicately colored images of cats, mice, frogs, and snatches of nursery rhyme, charms visitors. After years of redecoration and

In the nursery, two brass beds (of a type described by Clara as having been there) and a crib owned by the Clemenses are the places where Clara Clemens, Jean Clemens (in the crib), and a nursemaid would have slept in the early 1880s. The left-hand door leads to the room where Susy, old enough for her own room, slept. The other door leads to a bathroom. THE MARK TWAIN HOUSE & MUSEUM. PHOTOGRAPH BY JOHN GROO.

Recently restored, a crib used by Samuel and Livy Clemens for their children in the Hartford house was reportedly given to the Clemenses' cook, Katharine Duff, who passed it down in her family until it returned to the museum in the early 1940s.
THE MARK TWAIN HOUSE & MUSEUM, 1942.01. MUSEUM PURCHASE FROM JOSEPH F. DOWNING. PHOTOGRAPH BY ALANA BORGES GORDON.

multiple uses of this room (it was once the museum office), a scrap of the original paper was found behind the fireplace woodwork. The pattern was determined to be by the British artist Walter Crane, whose illustrations for children's books in a style heavily influenced by medieval and Japanese models were popular with parents of the era. A reproduction wallpaper was created as part of the restoration of the house. The pictures and words evoke an old British ballad, "Ye Frog He Would A-Wooing Go" (better known by U.S. visitors in its Appalachian version, "Froggy Went A-Courtin'"). In the nursery song, the wedding of Mr. Frog and Miss Mouse is cut short by murders perpetrated by a cat and a duck.

Too tragic for a nursery? In fact, cats were the adored lords and ladies of the Clemens hearths, with names such as Sour Mash, Zoroaster, and Blatherskite. The author was always deeply respectful of the animal: "If man could be crossed with the cat it would improve man, but it would deteriorate the cat." Another sign of the nonchalance with which the Victorians exposed their children to the reality of death is a pair of tiles over the fireplace displaying the funeral of Cock Robin. ("Who killed Cock Robin? I, said the Sparrow, with my bow and arrow, I killed Cock Robin.")

On August 16, 1883, Hay left the family. Samuel wrote to his mother:

> *Rosa went away today—to get married. She has been with us eleven years; & I believe this is the first time she has been away from us a day in that time. All the children are mourning for her—but poor Jean thinks she is coming back, & nobody undeceives her.*

The wallpaper in the nursery is by Walter Crane, a well-known British illustrator of children's books. The nursery illustrations portray scenes from the nursery rhyme "Ye Frog He Would A-Wooing Go," or its American variant, "Froggy Went A-Courtin'." Both versions have a gruesome ending, with the bride (a mouse) and her frog husband eaten by, respectively, a cat and a duck. Crane designed it for Jeffrey and Company, a London firm that also produced his friend William Morris's designs.
THE MARK TWAIN HOUSE & MUSEUM. PHOTOGRAPH BY JOHN GROO.

The Study and Schoolroom

As she proceeded through the house with Potter in 1874 and exclaimed about the charm of the nursery, Fairbanks mentioned the door from that room "into the father's study." The elegant, dark-paneled room, between the nursery and the suite provided for Livy's mother, was in fact used by Clemens as a study for the first six years that they lived in the house. Notable in it—along with heavy furniture decorated with gryphons and sphinxes—was a divan built into two sides of a right-angled corner by a set of windows, shown today strewn with Persian carpets and cushions. "There was a good idea," he told George Parsons Lathrop of *Harper's* magazine, "which I got from something I saw in a Syrian monastery."

A *New York Sun* reporter described the rest of the room in 1878:

> *It is a strange apartment. The floor was littered up with a confusion of newspapers, newspaper cuttings, books, children's toys, pipes, models of machinery, and cigar ends. Twain's method is to drop everything when he's done using it, but he will let nobody else interfere with the arrangements of his study. "I am naturally lazy," he says, "and I wish to conquer the detestable habit by imposing on myself a certain amount of domestic work. I take care of the room myself." In one corner stood a stack of his patent self-gumming scrapbooks. On the mantel, where the bust of Calvin stood until Mark destroyed it with a poker in a moment of religious frenzy, I noticed a pitcher that looked as if it contained beer. On the table were many manuscript sheets of Mr. Clemens's unfinished historical work, "The Mother-in-Law in All Ages."*

Other than the bust-of-Calvin story and the mother-in-law book, which have the ring of Twainian whimsy gleefully reported by an adoring reporter, this account seems true to life—right down to "Mark Twain's Patent Self-Pasting Scrap Book," which Clemens in fact patented in 1873. About twenty-five thousand of these had sold the year before the reporter's visit. Children's toys were noted by another reporter several years later—when Clemens had left the room to seek a study elsewhere. The reporter described

> *a large room fitted up most comfortable with cozy nooks filled in with cushioned seats. Beyond is a room [the nursery] in which a large rocking horse and scattered toys make one acquainted with the reason Mr. Clemens ceased writing in this attractive apartment and moved still further upstairs to a corner of the billiard room.*

Before he left, however, the study was the scene of a drama of master–servant relationships in the summer of 1877. Called back to Hartford from the family's summer retreat in Elmira, Clemens learned that Susy's English nursemaid Elizabeth Wills (known as "Lizzie") had been letting her boyfriend, Willie Taylor, into the house at night. As a result, she was pregnant, she tearfully told Clemens. The author took on the role of a furious father, called Taylor to the house, and here in the study demanded that he marry Wills. The alternative was to be arrested by a policeman waiting in the library on the first floor, who would collar him for burglary as he left the house. The purported father resisted:

> *He was raging up and down the room and trying to imagine some way to get out of those dreadful toils. I tried to interest him in that impending child. I made a moving appeal to his parental instincts and to his duty toward that blameless little creature, but it only raised his fury a couple of thousand degrees higher than it was before. He said he would allow no man's bastards to be foisted upon him.*

At last the man relented, and a second hidden participant, sweating from his long concealment in a stuffy neighboring bathroom, emerged—the Reverend Joseph Twichell, Clemens's close friend. The ceremony was performed, Clemens called for cake and wine, and he "gave each a check for $100 to start their life with," Twichell reported.

There was a sequel. Three years later, as Clemens told it, he saw a carriage stop in front of the house. "I noticed that there was a lady and a gentleman in it, he and that they were looking intently and apparently expectantly toward me. . . . The occupants of the carriage were finely and fashionably dressed and gloved, and the gentleman had on his head a silk hat which was as shiny as the coats of the horses." It was the Taylors, and Willie told Clemens that the forced marriage was "the greatest favor anybody ever did me." He went on:

> *I hadn't a cent; I hadn't any work; I hadn't a friend, and I couldn't see anything in front of me but the poor house. Well, [Lizzie] is the girl that has changed all that; she saved me, and I thank you again. She got work for me, all I could do . . . she started a little restaurant down in Main street, and got Mr. Bunce and Mr. Robinson and General Hawley and Mr. George Warner, and all your other influential friends who had known her in your house, to come and try her bill of fare. They liked it, and brought everybody else, and pretty soon she had all the custom she could attend to, and was making money like a mint, and it's still going on yet.*

And the child?

> *He paused; then he added, without any bitterness in his tone, "But as to that child, it hasn't ever arrived, and there wasn't the damnedest least prospect of it the time that she told you that fairy-tale—and never had been!"*

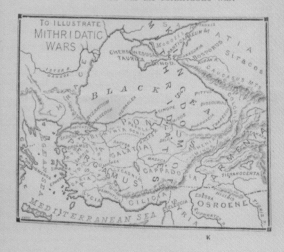

Livy recorded Susy's "brilliant recitation in Ancient History" in 1885. In the museum's collection is *Outlines of the World's History Ancient, Medieval and Modern,* by William Swinton, a book the thirteen-year-old may have used to prepare for this performance, with her own notes scrawled in the margins. THE MARK TWAIN HOUSE & MUSEUM, 371.32S979. PHOTOGRAPH BY JOHN GROO.

Clemens relished the tale, turning it into a work of fiction at one point. But he particularly relished the role of *deus ex machina* he was able to play in these people's lives.

When Clemens left the original study behind, it became Susy and Clara's schoolroom. This change has been tentatively dated from the arrival of both Jean and an upright piano in 1880. The piano was moved into the former study. Clara describes this piece as a Christmas present, perhaps prompted by her innocent question while watching her father play in the drawing room: "Do girls ever play?" The receipt for the piano notes that it came accompanied by twenty lessons.

Livy had done much of their teaching up to this point, possibly in the library or drawing room, as she reported a two-hour session when Susy was seven and Clara was five:

> *First we have a reading lesson in German—three or four pages of the German reader then Geography—a short lesson in that, then mental arithmetic, then they make numbers in their copy books . . . in the middle of the lessons somewhere we have bean bags or gymnastics, and one day they . . . sewed a little.*

German was important to the Clemenses—part of the reason for hiring Rosina Hay was to tutor the whole family in the language. The family traveled and lived in German-speaking countries; Samuel Clemens's struggles in learning the language led to a famous essay, "The Awful German Language," but his letters are full of German endearments for Livy and entire sections of family news rendered in a butchered version of the tongue.

With the schoolroom came new governesses, one of the most constant being Lilly Gillette Foote. Livy wrote in her journal, with the girls now eleven and thirteen years old, on "the last day of the children's examination":

> *Clara passed a most excellent examination in her Geography. Susy told the story of Cupid and Psyche in Latin, Miss Foote asking her questions. Susy gave what I think without partiality was a brilliant recitation in Ancient History. She talked for fully an hour. . . . Occasionally she would say well Miss Foote, the book says so and so, but it seems to me in this way, stating something quite different.*

Clara, for her part, recalled "memory tests of books we had read and hated." Katy Leary reported Saturday theatricals in this room—"They frequently played the balcony scene from 'Romeo and Juliet'"—with the sculptor Gerhardt painting the scenery and, as Clara said, "a larger cast of actors than auditors." This was also the place for the children to open Christmas gifts and, "best of all," said Clara, enjoy popcorn and roasted chestnuts cooked over the fire. The children made a few forays into the public school system—one of Clara's Hartford Public High School report cards gives her mediocre marks for academics and poor marks for behavior—but in general it was Miss Foote who provided their early education.

First Clemens's study and then, as portrayed in the house today, the schoolroom for the children. It is here that, Clara said, the girls were submitted to "memory tests of books we had read and hated." But they had triumphs, too, including dramatic performances with sets built by the Clemenses' sculptor protégé Karl Gerhardt and piano lessons.
THE MARK TWAIN HOUSE & MUSEUM. PHOTOGRAPH BY JOHN GROO.

The mantel in the schoolroom is piled with books in German—fluency in the language was considered an important aspect of the children's education—as well as a bell jar of stuffed birds and a portrait of Queen Victoria. This latter makes reference to the Clemenses' intense Anglophilia.
THE MARK TWAIN HOUSE & MUSEUM. PHOTOGRAPH BY JOHN GROO.

When Susy was six, her mother noted her difficulty in saying her prayers. When her mother asked her why, she said that Miss Foote had told her that the Native Americans had several gods. "This had led Susy to thinking," Clemens later wrote. She did not pray "in the same way" anymore, and her mother asked her to explain. The answer was pure Mark Twain or Livy Clemens in its keen intelligence: "Well, Mamma, the Indians believed they knew, but now we know they were wrong. By and by, it can turn out that we are wrong. So now I only pray that there may be a God and a Heaven—or something better."

Jean, as she grew older, had a function in the schoolroom theatricals that was described by Clemens himself:

> *The chief characters were always a couple of queens, with a quarrel in stock—historical, when possible, but a quarrel anyway, even if it had to be a work of imagination. Jean always had one function—only one. She sat at a little table about a foot high and drafted death warrants for the queens to sign.*

When Susy was eighteen, Clara sixteen, and Jean ten, in 1890, the family was only about a year away from what turned out to be a permanent departure from the house. Clemens, now in his fifties, still corresponded with Mary Fairbanks. He wrote about their educational prospects:

> *Susy is a freshman at Bryn Mawr . . . Clara decides to stay out of college and devote herself to music. Goes to New York twice a month & takes a lesson from an old & brilliant pupil of Liszt and Clara Schumann, who says she will pan out to admiration on the piano. She practices three hours a day. We haven't forecast Jean's future yet, but think she is going to be a horse jockey and live in the stable.*

THE THIRD FLOOR
George Griffin's Room

Climbing to the third floor of the house, still under construction, Potter and Fairbanks in their 1874 tour passed a door to a room that was later used by the butler George Griffin.

Griffin had great financial and political acumen, along with stringent moral habits, and was a "trusted political leader" in Hartford's African American community. "At any time after his first five years' service with us his check was good for $10,000," Clemens wrote. (Again, multiply by 25 to get an idea of Griffin's strong credit rating of $250,000.) And he could predict the Black community's vote in Hartford "to a man before the polls opened on election day." This could be a profitable endeavor for Griffin, who also spent so much time listening to prominent Hartford visitors discussing politics in the house that he could get inside information and place significant bets. "Added to all this, he could put a lighted candle in his mouth and close his lips upon it," Clemens wrote. "Consider the influence of a glory like that upon our little kids in the nursery."

The beloved Griffin had to leave the household when Clemens, not as savvy a businessman as his butler, moved his

"George was an accident," Clemens wrote of the butler George Griffin. "He came to wash some windows and stayed half a generation." For half a century or more, scholars at the Mark Twain House sought a photograph of Griffin; the image from which this detail is taken, discovered by Mark Twain scholar Kevin Mac Donnell in 1994, was greeted with celebration. COURTESY OF KEVIN MAC DONNELL, AUSTIN, TEXAS.

A servant's room restored: the room where George Griffin, the Clemenses' butler, stayed when he was at the house. (With a family in Hartford, he was a commuter butler but needed a place to stay when he served late at night when the Clemenses entertained.) The emphasis on the servants' life at the museum in recent years has broadened and deepened the view of nineteenth-century Hartford, particularly in the Clemens house. THE MARK TWAIN HOUSE & MUSEUM. PHOTOGRAPH BY JOHN GROO.

family from Hartford in 1891 because of financial difficulties. But he used his Hartford connections to get a position the Union League Club in New York City, where he acted as informal banker to both fellow waiters and the club members, and where Clemens later visited him. The plainly furnished room shown today—the first room restored with attention to the life of the servants as well as the Clemens family—was there for Griffin to bunk when he had to work late or rise early. He had a wife and family on Wells Street in Hartford, and he was "deacon and autocrat," in Clemens's words, of the African Methodist Episcopal Zion Church downtown on Pearl Street.

Three other rooms have entries from this hall, high and remote from the rest of the house. Clara recalled that she and Susy kept wild squirrels as pets in one small room, or imprisoned a pirate there, or (when the pirate died) kept St. Francis there, "who we hoped would tame the squirrels." The girls' imaginations were boundless.

The Artist's Friend's Room

This guest room may have derived its name from Samuel Clemens's mischievous delight in portraying himself as an artist. In *A Tramp Abroad*, his semi-fantastic account of the family's 1878–1879 tour of Europe, he said his plan was to study art there. His odd, primitive sketches adorn the book. Assigning the room to "the artist's friend" implies that this was a place for a male guest to retire after a late night of drinking and billiards. The double doors leading to the adjacent billiard room, so the two rooms could be combined into one large one, seem to confirm this notion. But it was empty much of the time. Clara wrote that "this room was so spooky that my sisters and I decided it was a suitable home for the insane wife of Rochester in *Jane Eyre*."

The Clemens portrait next to the billiard room door is by Dora Wheeler Keith, the daughter of Associated Artists principal and renowned interior designer Candace Wheeler. It reflects Clemens's appearance in 1889, when a *New York Times* reporter mentioned "his fine profusion of hair is silvering fast. . . . His mustache clings to its reddish hue, and his heavy eyebrows appropriately maintain a just equilibrium as to color."
THE MARK TWAIN HOUSE & MUSEUM, 1935.6.1. GIFT OF MRS. DORA WHEELER KEITH. PHOTOGRAPH BY JOHN GROO.

Spookiness and man-cave reputation aside, the room also was referred to as "the pink room," and for six weeks or so in 1887 it housed a decidedly feminine tenant: Aoki Koto House, the adopted daughter of Clemens's journalist friend—and later enemy—Edward H. House. House had settled in Japan, teaching and publishing Tokyo's first English-language newspaper. He adopted Koto, a former student of his, after a failed marriage had nearly driven her to suicide. In 1880, the father and daughter moved to America, and during visits to the Clemenses in Hartford, Koto was a particular favorite of the family. Clemens wrote after one such visit:

> Koto is gone—& freighted as usual, with everybody's hearts. She conquered right & left. . . . She had a large audience of random visitors, last night, & sat before them, and told them about Japanese customs, with the winning eloquence of her simple ways

The "artist's friend's room" was also known as the pink room or Koto's room, this last in honor of its tenancy by Japanese-born guest Aoki Koto, the adopted daughter of American journalist Edward H. House. House was a longtime associate of Clemens's, but the two split over the dramatic rights to *The Prince and the Pauper*. THE MARK TWAIN HOUSE & MUSEUM. PHOTOGRAPH BY JOHN GROO.

and gentle heart & truthful words, so captivated them, fascinated them, that Mrs. Clemens was "as proud of her as she could be." . . . And so we do all grant that Koto is the dearest & loveliest spirit that lives in this earth.

In 1890, a dispute over the dramatic rights to *The Prince and the Pauper* drove Clemens and Edward House apart permanently, and there were no more visits from Koto. But her stay in the third-floor guestroom gave it yet a third name: Koto's room.

The Billiard Room

Another room, in which you may look for the "author" when you find the study vacant—a billiard parlor with verandahs that look like turrets, from which to study the movements of the enemy.

—MARY MASON FAIRBANKS, 1874

The billiard room, with three doors leading to three separate high balconies, its windows streaming with light, is the high point of the home in more ways than architecturally. What went on here provides the reason why the house is preserved. It's the place where Samuel Clemens produced his vivid fictional creations or drew on his vast collection of notes to produce travel narratives, or prepared short pieces that still make us explode into laughter today, or wielded his "pen warmed-up in hell" when he saw injustice, irrationality, or cruelty that needed to be dealt with summarily. He wrote in other places—for example, in Elmira, in the small octagonal study his sister-in-law had built for him. He could

From his riverboat piloting days as a young man until the end of his life, Samuel Clemens played billiards, practiced billiards, socialized over billiards, and attended billiard tourneys. Here he ponders a shot in his New York apartment in 1908. He later scrawled a comment on the photo: "Oh, John the Baptist couldn't get a count out of an arrangement like that!" THE MARK TWAIN HOUSE & MUSEUM COLLECTIONS.

During the summer while he lived in Hartford, Clemens worked in an octagonal study his sister-in-law had built for him in Elmira, New York. He said he could write nine chapters during those family stays in Elmira for every one he could write in Hartford, where social engagements, business matters, and household affairs ate up much of his creative time. THE MARK TWAIN HOUSE & MUSEUM COLLECTIONS.

write nine chapters there for every one he could write in Hartford, he said. But he appears to have begun using this room for a refuge from his second-floor study even before the house was finished, as Fairbanks related as she reached this floor of the house with Potter.

A reporter once said of the room:

> *Its windows look to the westward over a festive and noisy brook in a setting of rich, green turf, past clumps of elm and birch and oak and maple. A long line of high blue hills marks the western border. On the other side of them is the Farmington Valley. Close at hand the robin's nests on a tall beech seem likely to fall in at the window. It is a delightful spot altogether, just the place for hard work.*

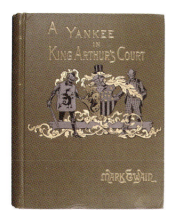 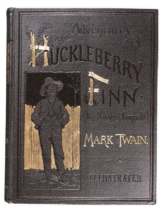 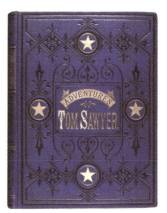 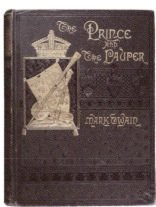

The years Samuel Clemens spent in Hartford were the years when he produced his best-known works. Aside from his productive Elmira summers, he sometimes sought literary refuge—in the carriage house barn or a friend's study down the street. But his billiard room–study was the place where he could work on revision, write hundreds of letters, and write the short pieces that still provoke laughter—or provide thoughtful insight—today. THE MARK TWAIN HOUSE & MUSEUM COLLECTIONS.

Though he didn't give up his "real" study until 1880, he was already using the room as a workplace while the building was being built. A plumber working on the house in 1874 reported that "sometime before the billiard room on the third floor was entirely finished Mark Twain was frequently seen to go there to spend his mornings writing." Three years later, Fairbanks asked him, "Where do you write?" "In the billiard room," he replied, "the most satisfactory study that ever was. Open fire, register, and plenty of light."

He had dreamed of a billiard room at the top of his home since long before he had met Livy or known Hartford. In the Nevada silver fields in the early 1860s, as he relates in *Roughing It*, he and his partner Calvin Higbie thought they'd struck it rich. "I thought I was worth a million dollars," he wrote—neither the first time nor the last time that he thought that. Living in a wooden shanty and quietly staking a claim on a genuinely rich vein of ore, he and Higbie planned what do with their wealth. "I was altering and amending the plans for my house, and thinking over the propriety of having the billiard-room in the attic, instead of on the same floor with the dining-room," Clemens wrote; "also, I was trying to decide between green and blue for the upholstery of the drawing-room, for, although my preference was blue I feared it was a color that would be too easily damaged by dust and sunlight." Shortly after this reverie, he and Higbie lost their claim on a technicality and returned to their customary poverty.

Billiards, business, and the creation of great literature—all were functions of the third-floor billiard room. (The literature was created at a table in the corner.) Here Clemens started working even as the house was being built and, in early years, retreated to work away from the bustle of the living spaces of the house. Finally, as his study was taken over as a schoolroom for good, this became his full-time work space. THE MARK TWAIN HOUSE & MUSEUM. PHOTOGRAPH BY JOHN GROO.

Wealth had come in a guise other than a vein of silver: from his marriage and from his skill with words. By 1889, he was at the peak of his prosperity when the *New York Times* came to call:

> *Mr. Clemens took his visitor on stairs to what appeared to be his sanctum and a billiard room combined. He had been standing at the billiard table writing. . . . He walked up and down the room smoking a wooden pipe, which had a chronic tendency to fall in two and required filling often. There was a writing desk in the room and a case full of books beside it. "Do you write at that desk Mr. Clemens?" "No, I write there." "There" was a small semi-circular table pushed up to the wall, strewn with papers and affording very little elbow room for writing. . . . "And when may I expect another book?" "I don't know," replied Mr. Clemens, "I don't write the book. A book writes itself. If there is another book in me, it will come out, and I will put it on paper." Thus the humorist's works pass through two stages of evolution. First there is a process of mental incubation. Then the work is transferred to paper and remains in a sort of chrysalis condition in pigeonholes until it is ripe for publication.*

Wooden "pigeonhole" shelves are there today, to the side of the billiard table, though not nearly as full as they seem to have been during Clemens's tenure in the house. It was there that the unfinished *Huckleberry Finn* manuscript sat while Clemens and his minister friend Twichell were rowing down the Neckar River in Germany, when Clemens turned the voyage into an imaginary raft trip and smashup. Twichell himself turned journalist a few years later, noting in *Harper's* magazine in 1896 that "quantities of manuscript lie in his pigeon holes that have never gone to the printer." By then the Clemenses had been living abroad for five years and were thinking of renting the house. Remembering these quantities of manuscripts, Clemens wrote his Hartford business agent, "If the Barneys take the house, please have the letters & MSS [manuscripts] in the pigeon-holes & table-drawers of the billiard room bundled up & stored out of reach in the reserved attic." Visitors note the striking decor of the room—the ceiling painted with cigar bundles, pipes, and billiard cues; the similar motifs on two translucent pieces of marble mounted in the wall like windows, with "C" for Clemens and numerals representing the year they moved into the house: "18" in one marble sheet, "74" in the other.

The room was a study but also a place for convivial gatherings around the billiard table. A speaking tube in the wall, like similar tubes in other rooms, led

The billiard room ceiling was emblazoned with images of masculine Victorian leisure: crossed billiard cues, billiard balls, pipes, and bundled cigars. Though these painted decorations were long gone when the house was restored in the 1960s and 1970s, wallpaper affixed to the ceiling, when removed, displayed faint images of the Clemens-era designs. Architect Edward Tuckerman Potter added translucent marble panels on either side of a glass door and windows leading out to a balcony. Both have the initial "C" for Clemens; the one on the left displays the number "18" and the other the number "74," for the date of the house: 1874. THE MARK TWAIN HOUSE & MUSEUM. PHOTOGRAPHS BY JOHN GROO.

to the kitchen on the first floor for communication with the servants. On June 6, 1884, a group of men including Clemens, his lawyer, his Hartford business manager, and three others were aiming their cues, listening to the gentle tap and roll of the balls, but also waiting for the whistle from the tube that would tell them important political news was coming up from below. They feared that the news would be bad.

The kitchen—two floors down—had a telephone mounted on a wall, and the butler Griffin was waiting there, between the phone and the speaking tube to the billiard room. At Exposition Hall in Chicago, the Republican Party was nominating a presidential candidate. These men in the billiard room, including Clemens, were staunch Republicans and all subscribed to the Republican paper, the *Hartford Daily Courant*. They feared that their party's choice would be

During the election of 1884, Clemens broke with the Republican Party after it nominated James G. Blaine, a notably corrupt candidate, for president. He voted for Democratic candidate Grover Cleveland. As he told the story, the news came to him and a group of friends in the billiard room, through one of the speaking tubes (such as the one shown here near the cue rack) from the kitchen. There, butler George Griffin was relaying the word he had gotten by telephone from the local Republican headquarters, which was in contact with the nominating convention in Chicago by telegraph. CLEVELAND AND BLAINE PORTRAITS: COURTESY OF THE LIBRARY OF CONGRESS. THE MARK TWAIN HOUSE & MUSEUM. PHOTOGRAPH BY JOHN GROO.

James G. Blaine of Maine, believed to be viciously corrupt in the lucrative congressional matter of granting land charters to railroad companies. "All these men were Republicans, but they had no affection for Blaine," Clemens wrote years later. "For two years, the Hartford Courant had been holding Blaine up to scorn and contumely."

About mid-afternoon, Griffin got the call from the Republican headquarters, where operatives were getting the news from Chicago by telegraph. He crossed to the speaking tube and blew into the whistle. In the billiard room upstairs, the men listened through the tube. Blaine had been nominated on the third ballot. "The butts of the billiard cues came down on the floor with a bump," Clemens wrote, "and for a while the players were dumb."

With that bump began a political drama in which Clemens and a few other prominent Republicans defied the party establishment and went for the Democratic candidate, Grover Cleveland. Clemens told his fellow billiard players that "no party held the privilege of dictating to me how to vote." He followed through and became a spokesman for the Independent Republicans in Hartford—the group later known as "mugwumps." This position set him at odds with his old friends at the *Courant*, which had about-faced and toed the official Republican line. When Clemens spoke at a rally for the Independent Republicans, the *Courant* did not deign to cover it, though up to that time the newspaper had hung on his every public word and act.

Hartford has a long memory and harbors its resentments. Clemens's gut instinct to follow his political conscience in this room on that day almost led to his house's destruction more than forty years later, when a *Hartford Courant* publisher remembered his betrayal of the Republican cause and criticized his own newspaper's efforts to save the building.

But for the man on the other end of the speaking tube—Griffin—this day provided an opportunity. Griffin bet heavily on Blaine, who was the clear favorite over Cleveland—there hadn't been a Democratic president since before the Civil War. Then, a week before the election, Blaine stumbled: an overzealous supporter labeled the Democrats the party of "rum, Romanism, and rebellion." This attack on Irish Americans' sobriety, religion, and patriotism was widely publicized by the Democrats and energized the Cleveland vote. Speaking of this slur, Clemens reports, "From one of his subsidized information sources George learned of it three hours before it had gotten currency in Hartford, and he let no grass grow under his feet. Within that time he had covered his Blaine bets with bets at two to one against him." Cleveland and Griffin were both winners on election day.

The Clemenses' future days in the house were dwindling by now, however. Another act of good faith in this same room three years earlier, in 1881, had sowed the seeds of the family's eventual departure from their Hartford house. Dwight Buell, who had sold jewelry to Livy from his shop on Main Street in Hartford, came to the door, was shown up to the billiard room, and made a proposition to Clemens that the author described somberly in his autobiography: "He wanted me to take some stock in a type-setting machine."

THE KITCHEN AND SERVANTS' WING

The visitor who accuses Mark Twain of disrespect to the avenue in putting the kitchen in front misleads you, although the humorous proprietor would justify such an arrangement on the ground that it would make his servants cheerful if they could overlook the funerals and St. Patrick's processions, while he would choose to gaze from his library windows upon the dainty pictures which nature will paint for him in all the colors of the changing seasons.

—Mary Mason Fairbanks, 1874

In June 1885, Susy, age thirteen, announced to the family, "I have been to the kitchen and it turns out we are to have Miss Corey & fish balls for breakfast." Susy's wonderful juxtaposition (Corey seems to have shared the duties of governess with Lilly Foote) amused Clemens enough to jot it down as one of the last entries in "A Record of the Small Foolishnesses of Susie and 'Bay' Clemens (Infants)," a running account of the children's funny and wise sayings he had kept since Susy was four. "Bay" was a nickname given Clara based on Susy's early pronunciation of the word "baby."

Out of the kitchen on the ground floor of the house came not only fish balls but also bountiful meals like the ones Grace King described—the Claire soup, the salmon, the broiled chicken, the tomato salad with mayonnaise (then a sauce prepared from scratch, not something from a jar), the Charlotte Russe, and cream and strawberries. The constant food preparation had begun from the time the family first moved in, when Clemens was clearly relieved that they could stop having to rely on the kitchens of others. He wrote of the cook Margaret Cosgrave, "Margaret's cookery goes ahead of anything we have had at the best table in New York."

The kitchen wing, which visitors approach via the back stairs much as a housemaid might have, is one of the more recent restorations to the house. It was used for offices until 2003, when these were vacated with the opening of the new Visitor Center. With almost no contemporary descriptions and no photographs to go by, the museum relied on "building archaeology." A team of specialists was hired to probe within the walls and find signs of what might have been there. They discovered what the Twain-era floors looked like, the color the walls were painted, how the woodwork was finished, and how the rooms were partitioned. They discovered features long hidden and forgotten (such as a dumbwaiter and pass-throughs) and the location of sinks, gas light

It was in the kitchen that the vast number of meals needed for a family of five and their six to seven servants were prepared, along with a legion of guests. One meal recorded seems to have had cream as a major element: "shad roe balls with cream shad sauce, asparagus with cream sauce (on toast), roast lamb with cream curry sauce and peas," and, of course, "strawberries in cream." Not for nothing had Livy in 1876 bought property across the Little River from the house for an extra cow pasture. THE MARK TWAIN HOUSE & MUSEUM. PHOTOGRAPH BY JOHN GROO.

fixtures, and speaking tubes. Then careful restoration was done, and the result is what you see: most prominently, the great black Cyrus Carpenter & Co. coal stove, which followed a shape visible on the stripped-down brick chimney after the century of alterations and adjustments. The Clemens-era paint was carefully matched, and auxiliary rooms were re-created. There was a pantry, today supplied with canned goods and stoneware beer bottles, along with a prominent wire mousetrap; a scullery, the place where dishes were washed in water heated by running it through the stove and into a gleaming copper tank; and a "sink room" that provided an intermediate staging area for the food to be passed to the butler's pantry. This would be done via a pass-through in the wall, where, in Griffin's domain, the food would be transferred to the family's best serving bowls. Griffin himself would carry the platters into the dining room for presentation at the table.

When visitors today get to the kitchen, they hear more about Griffin and Leary. They learn of John and Ellen O'Neil, gardeners and caretakers after the Clemenses left the house. And of the coachman Patrick McAleer, who had been with the Clemenses since their marriage: "Patrick the coachman was part of our wedding outfit.... He was Irish, young, slender, bright, quick as a cat, a master of his craft.... He had long foresight, and a memory which was so good that he never seemed to forget anything." Fifteen years after leaving Hartford, Clemens returned to be a pallbearer at McAleer's funeral.

And there were "birds of passage," Clemens said—"servants who tarried a while, were dissatisfied with us or we with them, & presently vanished out of our life, making but slight impression upon it for good or bad."

(Opposite page) In a southward view of the kitchen, the door to a hall leading to the dining room provides a glimpse of the servants' early morning route into the house to perform chores that were not finished until long after dark. Adjoining it is the butler's pantry, the domain of George Griffin, the Clemenses' indefatigable butler (and a major figure in Hartford's African American community). He had the privilege of handling the finest china, crystal, and silver in the family's collection and waiting on their dining table. The elegant woodwork and glass of the cabinets in this room follow the curve of the outside wall of the house at this point. THE MARK TWAIN & MUSEUM. PHOTOGRAPHS BY JOHN GROO.

CHAPTER FIVE
"The House Is Still Full of Carpenters"

HAVING TAKEN A TOUR THROUGH ALL THE YEARS the Clemenses lived in the house, by means of our visit to all the rooms, we now travel back to the beginning of their time there, in September 1874, five months after Mary Fairbanks took her own tour with the architect Potter.

They had spent those months in Elmira, where they were surprised by another construction altogether at Quarry Farm, the residence of Livy's sister Susan Crane and her husband Theodore. About one hundred yards uphill from the house, their hosts had had built an ornate octagonal study for Clemens, high on a hilltop, designed by Potter's associate Alfred H. Thorp. It seems the country cousin of the Hartford house, the jigsaw work around the edge of its roof angled as though whipped by the wind, like the similar work around the edge of the roof of the third-floor Hartford house balcony—also octagonal, and one of the house's most prominent features. Clemens wrote Twichell:

> *It sits in perfect isolation on top of an elevation that commands leagues of valley & city & retreating ranges of distant blue hills . . . & when the storms sweep down the remote valley & the lightning flashes among the hills beyond, & the rain beats upon the roof over my head, imagine the luxury of it!*

It would provide a place for uninterrupted summer days of work during the whole time the Clemenses lived in Hartford. On June 8, Clara was born.

Clemens kept in touch with the house-building project through the family attorney. In July, he visited Hartford to see how the work was progressing and to straighten out difficulties that had developed among the general contractor, John Garvie; the landscaper, Charles Macrae; and Potter. He apprised Livy, "I have reminded Garvie to obey Potter's orders. Have blown up Mr. McCray

During his last visit to Elmira with Livy in 1903, Clemens has a look out the window of his octagonal study. The building was later moved to the campus of Elmira College, about three miles from its original hilltop site, and can be visited today. THE MARK TWAIN HOUSE & MUSEUM COLLECTIONS.

& told him not to offend again by taking orders from anybody but Mr. Potter." He reported the amount of money that had been spent on "house, grounds, barn & architect" as $40,000. He likewise reported on the ubiquitous visitors: "Small processions of people continue to rove through the house all the time." And then he waxed lyrical:

> You may look at the house & grounds from any point of view you choose, and they are exquisite. It is a quiet, murmurous, enchanting poem done in the solid elements of nature. The house & the barn do not seem to have been set up on the grassy slopes & levels by laws & plans & specifications—it seems as if they grew up out of the ground and were part and parcel of Nature's handiwork.

The Mark Twain House in its full glory. Its positioning reminds many visitors of the general stance of a steamboat, with its extended porch resembling the main deck and the third-floor balcony resembling a pilot house. Clemens did make nautical references to elements of the house. The porch, or *ombra*, was also "the deck," and he referred to the "port" and "starboard" sides of the billiard room. But there seems to be no evidence that the house was planned that way, as some have claimed. THE MARK TWAIN HOUSE & MUSEUM. PHOTOGRAPH BY JOHN GROO.

(Opposite page) The decorated brick and the elaborate woodwork of the house, here seen at its south end where the conservatory dominates the ground floor, put it strongly into the tradition of Victorian architecture. The designs of the time included disparate elements that later generations saw as clashing and peculiar, but which have come back into favor in more recent decades.
THE MARK TWAIN HOUSE & MUSEUM. PHOTOGRAPH BY JOHN GROO.

The general contractor's brother, Robert Garvie, worked on the house's plumbing. In 1935, when he was eighty-eight, he described Clemens's visits to the site as generally placid, "making suggestions and conferring with the architect," but "he was impetuous and I have seen him very angry, especially when things went wrong about the building plans." The builders teased a group of young girls who visited from Miss Porter's School in Farmington, telling them the wood of the doors came from "a strange island in the South Seas once visited by Mark Twain" and grudgingly giving them scraps of it. Like the thousands of schoolchildren who visit the house today, if less orderly, the girls "ran about the place examining every nook and corner from cellar to garret." Clemens reported from his July 1874 visit that "the mulberry tree is flourishing." This was an

The drama of the brickwork and woodwork of the house continues on the north side of the structure, where porches open second- and third-floor rooms to the open air. Central to the scene is the kitchen wing of the house, which was the servants' realm; the "back stairs" were highly decorated on the exterior. Scholar Sarah Landau located a similar medieval enclosed staircase in a courtyard in France; it may have served as an inspiration to architect Potter. THE MARK TWAIN HOUSE & MUSEUM. PHOTOGRAPH BY JOHN GROO.

attempt for a link with authorial greatness; the tree had been planted from a cutting Clemens picked up in Stratford-upon-Avon during the England trip of the year before. It was supposed to be descended from a tree Shakespeare planted himself. The transplant was not a success. Though the tree survived, Clemens later wrote, "every June she would put out five or six pallid little buds, about the size of seed pearls, & leave them so till we had called witnesses and verified the fact, then she would take them in & save them for next year."

From Elmira, anticipating moving in September, he wrote to a friend, "The house does not look large, but has a modest aspect. It is on high ground, & in such a glorious breezy place, overlooking a sloping bank, with a small running brook at the base. Ah my boy, you must come."

Finally, on the rainy afternoon of September 19, 1874—after spending a week in New York to buy carpets and furniture, and so Clemens could attend rehearsals for his play based on *The Gilded Age*—they moved in. Along with them were Rosina Hay, the children's nursemaid, and Margaret Cosgrove, a cook whose work, Clemens wrote, "goes ahead of anything we have had at the best table in New York." The next day Clemens could write, "We are in part of the new house. Goodness knows when we'll get in the rest of it—full of workmen yet."

> *We have taken up quarters on the second story, sleeping in a guest room, eating in a nursery and using my study for a parlor—making the suite habitable and comfortable by using odds and ends of furniture that belong everywhere else in the house. And we are comfortable—when the banging of the hammers stops for a while.*

The comfort didn't last. A few days later, he wrote to Livy's family:

> *I have been bullyragged all day by the builder, by his foreman, by the architect, by the tapestry devil who is to upholster the furniture, by the idiot who is putting down the carpets, by the scoundrel who is setting up the billiard-table (& has left the balls in New York), by the wildcat who is sodding the ground & finishing the driveway (after the sun went down), by a book agent, whose body is in the back yard & the coroner notified.*

Observing the near-completed celebrity home on Farmington Avenue, the press had a good time. Houses in Hartford, says Clemens biographer Albert Bigelow Paine, were "mainly of the goods-box form of architecture, perfectly square, typifying the commercial pursuits of many of their owners." This was no goods box. The arrangement of gables, turrets, chimneys, and balconies—no two alike—gave the impression that Clemens described of having grown from the hillside above the stream. Many of the early descriptions called it straightforwardly "an English-style house," but the detail was from many sources. Certainly, the jigsaw and brickwork of the exterior—pierced boards with butterfly and floral and more abstract patterns, colored bricks set at various angles—had nothing to do with the English country architecture that the chimneys and gables might evoke, or the long, covered porch, stretching southward from the building into an *ombra*. The architectural term is derived from the Italian for "shade," and it allowed the Clemenses, when sitting on their wicker furniture set on ornate Asian carpets laid there by the

The function of the supporting beams on the *porte cochère* is fully visible, giving it a link, in the eyes of architectural historian Vincent Scully, to the movement he calls the "stick style" that led ultimately to Frank Lloyd Wright. But the leafy detail and cut-out butterflies put this building squarely in the High Victorian Gothic of the 1870s.
THE MARK TWAIN HOUSE & MUSEUM. PHOTOGRAPHS BY JOHN GROO.

servants, to peek around the side of the house and take in the view: hillside, stream, distant meadows, and the hazy mountains, the glass conservatory adding a picturesque detail in the foreground.

Some just saw the building as a crazy reflection of its humorist occupant: "It is built of brick, which material enters into its composition in every possible position," said a description reprinted in the Elmira newspaper. "The red parallelograms stand end-wise, side-wise, corner-wise, projecting here, depressed there, and ornamented nowhere. It is a small brick-kiln gone crazy, the outside ginger breaded with woodwork, as a baker sugar-ornaments the top and side of a fruit loaf." The paper even criticized Livy's decision to face the entry east and took a swipe at the Irish, as was common in Protestant discourse: "The house has evidently followed the Irish general's command of 'front to the rear,' and although the position puts a beautiful grove in the front, it leaves the kitchen with its barn wall and no windows only a couple of yards from the street." A Hartford paper called it simply "one of the oddest looking buildings in the State ever designed for a dwelling, if not in the whole country."

The description of the multicolored brickwork is not too far off the mark, though, and mirrors a poem attributed to Mark Twain himself in the Travelers Insurance Company's in-house publication of the era:

> *This is the house that Mark built.*
> *These are the bricks of various hue*
> *And shape and position, straight and askew,*
> *With the nooks and angles and gables too,*
> *Which make up the house presented to view,*
> *The curious house that Mark built.*

Clemens, living with his family on the second floor of the house in the fall of 1874, was tired of the carpenters' racket. He wrote his friend and editor at the *Atlantic Monthly*, William Dean Howells:

> *I have one or two things in my head that might do for the January number, perhaps, but the trouble is I can't hope to get them out while the house is still full of carpenters. So we'll give it up. These carpenters [he crossed out "dammit" here] are here for time & eternity; I am satisfied of that. I kill them when I get opportunities, but the builder goes & gets more.*

To another friend in October:

> *We have been in a portion of our house a month, & we expect the carpenters to give up the rest before Christmas—though "art is long" & so they may possibly remain with us a year or two more.*

And to another:

> *We are in our new house—& so are the carpenters—but we shall get the latter out, by & by, even if we have to import an epidemic to do it.*

On the morning of October 24, he wrote Howells again. He was still dry on a subject for an article in the January *Atlantic*, he said: "We are in such a state of weary and restless confusion that my head won't 'go.'" Then, in the afternoon, he wrote Howells once more:

> I take back the remark that I can't write for the Jan. number. For Twichell and I have had a long walk in the woods and I got to telling him about old Mississippi days of steamboat glory & grandeur as I saw them (during five years) from the pilot house. He said, "What a virgin subject to hurl into a magazine!" I hadn't thought of that before.

Thus began the writer's focus not only on the Mississippi of his piloting days but also on the Mississippi of his youth. In the following years, as he and Livy, the children, servants, and friends lived out their happy, stormy, angry, and imaginative lives in the Hartford house, Clemens turned out "Old Times on the Mississippi," the series for the *Atlantic*; the book *Life on the Mississippi* that grew out of it; and finally the books based on his childhood experiences in Hannibal, renaming childhood associates (mixed with a bit of himself and a healthy dose of invention) as Tom Sawyer and Huckleberry Finn.

Patrick McAleer, the Clemenses' longtime coachman, waits on Farmington Avenue in front of the completed Hartford house in the 1870s. The way the house faced to the side rather than the front was a matter of comment for the many observers. THE MARK TWAIN HOUSE & MUSEUM COLLECTIONS.

The carpenters at last departed, and Clemens found some peace on the balcony off the billiard room, which seems to have become a place of refuge for both husband and wife.

> *We have just got home again, middle of afternoon, and Livy has gone to rest and left the west balcony to me. There is a shining and most marvelous miracle of cloud-effects mirrored in the brook; a picture which began with perfection, and has momentarily surpassed it ever since, until at last it is almost unendurably beautiful. . . . There is a cloud-picture in the stream now whose hues are as manifold as those in an opal and as delicate as the tintings of a seashell. But now a muskrat is swimming through it and obliterating it with the turmoil of wavelets he casts abroad from his shoulders.*

Potter continued tying up loose ends in early 1875: "I should like to know when the stairbuilder gets the work up he has in hand, so I may see him at the house before he is quite finished up & to make sure that every thing is right. . . . If the red paint on the house isn't toning down, I wish to attend to it also." He discussed whether Verona blinds or awnings would be best to keep the sun out, what to do with the newel post at the bottom of the staircase, and whether to insert marble panels with a bas-relief of scenes from Washington Irving's "The Legend of Sleepy Hollow" over the mantel in the front hall. But by the early months of 1875, the house and the similarly styled carriage house to the south of the main house were essentially done.

What had they spent for it all—house, carriage house, and property? It is a question that visitors often ask, and the answer is not entirely clear. Clemens reported various figures—$110,000, $120,000, $157,000, $167,000—toward the end of his life when he was considering what to sell it for, but these seem exaggerated even if later alterations, decorations, and furnishings are added in. (There was significant work done on the house in 1881.) In mid-1874, he gave a progress report to Livy with a figure of $40,000, but the carpenters were there for a long time after that. The most thorough study of the cost was done by Walter K. Schwinn, president of the Mark Twain Memorial from 1965 to 1970. Schwinn wrote a manuscript history of the house that is kept in the museum's archives. In a full chapter he details the various land purchases involved, along with the evidence of city land records and other documentation. The closest to an accurate figure, he decided, was the value the city gave the property in 1877, two years after the house was completed. This was a figure that a landowner had to swear to, and Livy—in whose name the title was held—was not

Approaching the house from the south—in the 1870s, from the direction of George and Lilly Warner's house, today from the museum's Visitor Center—you pass the brick carriage house and barn, which Potter designed as a companion piece to the house. Coachman McAleer and his wife and five children lived in the wing extending from the barn area to the left. THE MARK TWAIN HOUSE & MUSEUM. PHOTOGRAPH BY JOHN GROO.

one to forswear herself: The city recorded $66,650. Again, multiply by roughly 25 to get that value in terms of today's dollars—about $1.66 million. (Of course, this "25 times" rule, and others cited, provides the roughest of equivalencies in light of what people earned in the era. A male laborer might earn $1.50 a day, a female cotton factory worker 75¢ to $2. In the middle class, salaries might be $3,000 a year for a minister or $6,000 a year for an army surgeon. In the Clemens household, Griffin made $360 a year in 1877; for comparison, the cook made $240, and the coachman $600, plus a dwelling attached to the carriage house. The housemaids made $150 or $155, with room and board.)

Finally, there is a story that Clemens asked the architect to make at least part of the house look like a steamboat. This story probably originated from an obvious source: When you stand on the lawn southeast of the house and look upward at the large, third-story octagonal balcony, with the *ombra* extending below it, it can reasonably be thought to look like a pilot house looming over the flat forward deck of one of the Mississippi crafts that Clemens piloted in his youth. He certainly enjoyed nautical analogies—the caption accompanying an illustration for an 1896 story in *Harper's* magazine calls the *ombra* "The Deck." Clemens also used the language of navigation to describe his worktable in the billiard room: "My table lay two points off the starboard bow of the billiard table, & the door of exit and entrance bore northeast-&-by east-half-east from that position."

But none of this implies intention. The story that the house was purposefully designed to look like a steamboat came from a journalist, insurance executive, and compiler of a massive history of Connecticut, Charles W. Burpee, who said in the 1920s that Potter had told him in the 1890s that Clemens had required Potter in the 1870s "to get some suggestions of a steamboat into the Clemens house." But this claim is tenuous, and other factors cast doubt on the idea. Pilot houses were square, not octagonal; steamboats were white, not red; and, according to the architectural historian Sarah Bradford Landau in her dissertation on Potter, if Clemens "had wanted steamboat imagery applied to his house, he would have had it applied quite explicitly." Potter was not subtle about imagery, she says, noting the Colt six-shooter bas-reliefs on his Church of the Good Shepherd and the cues and balls on the translucent marble panels in the Clemens billiard room.

The final verdict may come from an actual, licensed Mississippi steamboat pilot who visited the house in the 1960s. Richard Bissell (a very distant relative of the Bissells who eventually bought the Clemens house) was a quirky author from Iowa who wrote the novel on which the musical *The Pajama Game* was based. After his visit to Hartford, he wrote of the steamboat claim that he had "protested, and even got the curator to cease and desist from this allegation and to go stand in a corner." The idea that the house was designed to look like a steamboat, he said, was "invented by desperate journalists who have never been any closer to a Mississippi steamboat than the precinct rumshop."

CHAPTER SIX
"O Never Revamp a House!"

"YOU SUGGESTED WE LET UP ON THE FANCY TOUCHES till we knew how things were going to turn out," Potter wrote to Clemens around the time he finished working on the house in 1875, and in fact the walls of many of the rooms remained plainly decorated for the next few years simply because there was no money to continue the work. Even the beneficence of Olivia Lewis Langdon could go only so far, and the now-celebrated writer's income was not always reliable, despite the success of *Tom Sawyer*. This success was undercut by copyright infringement by Belford Brothers, a Canadian publisher, which flooded the American market with cheap knockoffs. Clemens wrote his English publisher, "This piracy will cost me $10,000, & I will spend as much more to choke off those pirates, if the thing can be done."

The Clemenses took a while to settle down in Hartford. Initially, Samuel was mistrusted by some of the elite as a Western boor. He sensed this attitude, and it stung. In her essay on his anxiety as he adjusted to the Hartford scene, "Mark Twain's Music Box," scholar Kerry Driscoll describes a December 1876 visit from Isabella Beecher Hooker, the Clemenses' former landlady, now their neighbor. The visit "took an acrimonious turn due to a pointed remark she made regarding one of the couple's recent purchases." Driscoll quotes Hooker's diary:

> *I had an unfortunate interview with Mr. C. I joked with him about not caring for a pretty lampshade after he had found it so very cheap—& he was vexed & said something about things going around the neighborhood & explained that he had no taste or judgment himself & so when an established house said a thing was good & charged a good price for it he felt sure that it was worthy of Livy & that was all he cared for.*

Driscoll continues:

> *Visibly discomfited at both the apparent scrutiny to which this insignificant object has been subjected as well as his neighbor's meddlesome stance as a self-appointed arbiter of household aesthetics, the writer blurts out an extraordinary confession—that he himself possesses "no taste or judgment"—and must therefore rely upon an extrinsic authority (in this case, a reputable merchant) in order to validate a thing's worth.*

Hooker pressed the point and wrote that Clemens's "eyes flashed and he looked really angry." It took Livy's—"Gravity's"—intervention to smooth things over. As Driscoll concludes, "much more is at stake in this conversation than a mere lampshade . . . Hooker is impugning his lack of both taste and sophistication."

These were creative years, however—the years of not only *Tom Sawyer* and *Huckleberry Finn* but also *The Prince and the Pauper* and some other, less successful attempts at playwriting. *The Innocents Abroad* remained his bestseller, and in the late 1870s he contracted with his publisher for another travel book.

The travels the Clemenses took in Europe in 1878–1879 had two other purposes: to engage the family in a program of art and language study devised by Livy and to acquire items for the Hartford house. They took careful measurements of the house beforehand, so they would know what size furniture to buy. Clemens extended a tape across the dining room:

> *Livy dear*
> *Dining Room*
> *From library door to window = 53 in.*
> *to hall door = 55½ in.*
> *sideboard to china closet door = 44 in.*
> *sideboard to window = 39½ in.*

From Europe, Livy wrote letters to her mother expressing gratitude for what seemed an unending stream of generosity. While Rosina Hay watched the children, she browsed in shops, as in Baden-Baden in August 1878, when she wrote to her mother:

> *Oh this is such a pretty town. The little shops are so very attractive, just think of shopping outdoors, how I do wish that I could give you some idea of these shops—the counters are right on the side walks so that you can do your errands without stopping inside the door.*

Or in Venice in October: "We have bought several most beautiful pieces of wood & I am very anxious to see them in our house—there is now standing in the room a carved chest that I have bought for our hall." And in "old curiosity shops," she wrote, "among lots of rubbish you find a great deal that you would want to own." In Milan in November, Clemens bought an Impressionist watercolor of a young girl by Daniele Ranzoni, the painting later to figure in the library storytelling games as "Emmeline." And it was during this period that they bought the angel-studded black walnut bed.

In February 1879, Livy began worrying about the backdrop to all these new acquisitions. In another letter to her mother, she wondered "whether we better decorate our house before we settle it or not. . . . What do you think about it Mother?" Olivia Langdon responded by offering them $1,000 for the work, evoking a letter from Livy expressing protest—and gratitude.

When they returned, they engaged an Elmira decorator named Frederick Schweppe, who seems, among other decorative touches, to have decorated the nursery, papering it with the Walter Crane illustrations to "Ye Frog He Would A-Wooing Go." "The nursery is perfect," Livy wrote to her mother, adding that "the house is exceedingly pretty and so wonderfully improved."

There remained, however, the highly public ground-floor rooms of the house. For this project, which started in early 1881 and kept the household in a disruptive state for a year, the Clemenses brought in some heavy guns.

First, there was some rebuilding to be done. "We have . . . set architect and builder to tear down our kitchen and build a new one," Clemens wrote his sister in March; "in June we shall tear out the reception room to make the front hall bigger; and at the same time the decorators will decorate the walls and ceilings of our whole lower floor." The family got back in touch with Potter, whose assistant Thorp would supervise the work, with the sometimes-fractious John Garvie again the general contractor. As they had when they were building the house, the Clemenses left town in the midst of a complicated project, spending the summer on the Connecticut shore and in Elmira. Clemens wrote furious letters from a distance against what he thought were overcharges by Garvie—"it can't cost $6,000 to build that 20 foot coop," he raged over the kitchen expansion. Livy, for her part, disagreed with Thorp over the amount of glass needed in the hall windows—she wanted more (visitors today still note what a dark room it is) and he wanted less. When the final bills came in, they appealed to Potter, who had retired from the complicated business of architecture and touchy clients several years earlier—or thought he did. Potter promised to help them out with Thorp over his bill and said he would forego his own fee.

The decoration of the front hall, where today the faux mother-of-pearl stenciling makes such a strong visual impression on the visitor, seems to have gone more smoothly. The Clemenses contacted Herbert M. Lawrence, a decorator who had done work for their friends, the Cheney silk family of Manchester. Lawrence was in Europe but recommended a number of alternatives, including "Mr. Louis Tiffany."

Tiffany was the son of the founder of the great New York jeweler, Charles Tiffany, but seems to have been more fun than his somewhat straitlaced father, frequenting the nightspots of Broadway with the architect Stanford White—who designed the Washington Square arch and was later shot to death by a jealous husband—and James Steele MacKaye, a theater manager, playwright, actor, and inventor who devised the idea of folding theater seats. In 1879, Tiffany had collected a small group of similarly minded designers together—Samuel Colman, Lockwood de Forest, and Candace Wheeler—in a venture called Associated Artists, which during its short tenure decorated, along with the Clemens house, the Madison Square Theater (for MacKaye), the Seventh Regiment Armory on Park Avenue, and a room in the White House.

Some pierced brass plates used around the fireplace in the entrance hall apparently came from de Forest's workshops in Ahmedabad, India, near Bombay. (De Forest wrote, "When I reached Ahmedabad . . . and saw street after street of carved houses and the many beautiful mosques of yellow sandstone, also elaborately carved, with their wonderful tracery windows, I made up my mind to have copies made of some of them no matter what difficulties I had to meet.")

But it was Candace Wheeler who had the longest association

Even after the 1881 alterations and decorations, the red-painted marble fireplace surround in the entry hall needed to be integrated with the detailing of the adjacent carved wood. In 1883, Clemens suggested that it be covered "with Mr. De Forest's thin arabesque cut brass sheets, which will let the red show through," and asked for some samples to experiment with—and the price. The $49 sheets are still in place today. THE MARK TWAIN HOUSE & MUSEUM. PHOTOGRAPH BY JOHN GROO.

Candace Wheeler had an important role in the 1881 redecoration of the main floor and stairwell halls of the Clemenses' home. Known as a textile and wallpaper designer, she was part of Louis C. Tiffany & Co., Associated Artists, and later took over the partnership entirely. In 1893, when this picture was taken, she was the decorator of the Woman's Building at the Chicago World's Fair and a Clemens family friend. THE MARK TWAIN HOUSE & MUSEUM COLLECTIONS.

with the Clemenses. Like Potter (who spent his retirement years devising ways to get sunlight into the mass housing in New York City that had been given the name "tenement"), she brought a social conscience to her work. She had no formal training before visiting the Woman's Building at the vast Centennial Exhibition in Philadelphia in 1876 (whose president was the Nook Farm resident, *Hartford Courant* co-owner, and Republican stalwart Joseph Hawley). There she saw work exhibited by the Royal School of Needlework in South Kensington, London, formed as part of a movement to fuse aesthetic ideals and the betterment of society. This effort was inspired by the designer William Morris, who took time off from designing his famed floral wallpaper patterns and textiles to distribute socialist tracts at mass meetings. George Bernard Shaw told Clemens years later that Morris was a confirmed "Huckfinnomaniac."

Wheeler examined the embroidery at the Exhibition—there were portraits of Queen Victoria and Prince Albert to admire, along with an elaborate picture in wool on canvas, "Death of George Douglas at the Battle of Langside"—and was inspired. She saw the possibilities of a similar American program for women who were "ashamed to beg and untrained to work" and sought to develop "the common and inalienable heritage of feminine skill in the use of the needle into a means of art-expression and pecuniary profit."

To achieve this end, she established the Society of Decorative Art in New York in 1877 and then, in the following year, established a Women's Exchange to help women sell work that they produced at home. With the invitation from Tiffany for a purely profit-making venture ("but art is there all the same," he assured her), she joined the Associated Artists with a specialty in textile design. She became head of the firm after Tiffany left it, making it an all-woman organization, famed for its textile and wallpaper designs, and

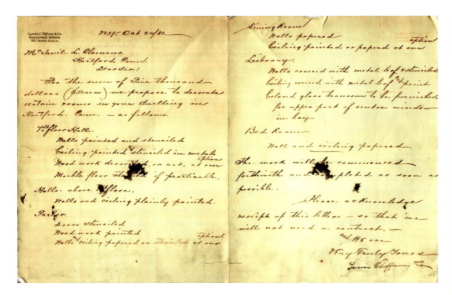

Another decorator who couldn't take the job steered the Clemenses toward Louis C. Tiffany, the son of the great New York jeweler, who formed Associated Artists before leaving to pursue his better-known career as a designer in glass and ultimately as Tiffany & Co.'s design director. Tiffany's letter serving as a contract with Clemens was gloriously unspecific: "Walls papered and stenciled; Ceiling papered and stenciled in metals; Woodwork decorated or not, at our option." PHOTOGRAPH: THE MARK TWAIN HOUSE & MUSEUM. GIFT OF MR. AND MRS. COLLIER PLATT. CONTRACT: COURTESY OF THE MARK TWAIN PAPERS AND PROJECT.

was visited by the likes of actress Lillie Langtry and author Oscar Wilde when they were in New York. She founded an artistic community at Onteora, in New York's Catskill Mountains, and when another great American exhibition came around—the Columbian Exposition of 1893 in Chicago—she was in charge of decoration for the Woman's Building. Her daughter Dora Wheeler was among the decorators for the building (another was the artist Mary Cassatt). The family remained close to the Clemenses, and the Clemenses visited Onteora. Dora Wheeler painted the picture of Clemens that hangs outside the billiard room on the Hartford house's third floor.

When Tiffany reached his agreement with Clemens in 1881, the plan for the front hall was put briefly: "Walls painted and stenciled; Ceiling painted and stenciled in metals; Woodwork decorated or not, at our option. . . . Halls above the first floor; Walls and ceilings plainly painted." The work as it stands today is hardly plain, adding the magic of a Persian palace to the front hall, the silver paisleys of a sari design to the drawing room, and further stencils adding glitter and mystery through the halls and stairwell up to the third floor. The work once again restricted the Clemenses to one portion of the house, starting in October when they returned from Elmira and lasting until Christmas Day. Clemens wrote, "We have all reached home & are living in a couple of rooms, the rest of the house being in the hands (indefinitely) of carpenters &c. . . . O never revamp a house! Leave it just as it was, & then you can economise in profanity."

CHAPTER SEVEN
"I Wish There Was Some Way to Change Our Manner of Living"

THE NEXT DECADE FOR THE CLEMENSES WAS characterized by an increasing number of investments in the Paige compositor, the typesetting device Clemens had first heard about in the billiard room from the jeweler Dwight Buell. "An old practical typesetter like myself can perceive the value of the thing," he wrote, putting $5,000 into the venture initially. "This typesetter does not get drunk," he wrote in his notebook. "He does not join the printer's union. A woman can operate him." He was called on for further investments as the inventor, James W. Paige, refined the endlessly difficult machine. At the same time, he entered the publishing field, founding Charles L. Webster & Co. (named for his partner, a nephew by marriage). Webster published *Adventures of Huckleberry Finn*, finally taken out of its billiard room pigeonhole and completed, and *Personal Memoirs of U. S. Grant*, a book of which Clemens, the ex-Confederate, was tremendously proud. Grant wrote it as he was dying from throat cancer—his taste for cigars exceeded Clemens's—but its massive sales ensured the financial well-being of his widow. Clemens kept the cancelled royalty checks for $150,000 and $200,000, made out to Julia Grant, displayed in the billiard room, where reproductions hang in their place today. The Paige typesetter, too, is on display, looming over the exhibit on Clemens's life in the Visitor Center as it loomed over this final decade in the Hartford house.

The future still seemed prosperous and contented in the early 1880s. Clemens had established his own fortune and fame, and the household no longer needed Langdon beneficence to keep it going. Kenneth R. Andrews, the most detailed chronicler of Nook Farm, described home life on one summer evening, June 13, 1885, using Livy's diary for detail:

> They ate an early dinner on the ombra. Afterwards, while it was still light, Patrick McAleer, who had been the Clemens's coachman from the Buffalo days, drove the long carriage from the stables to the porte-cochère so that the family of five could embark for a sunset drive. The carriage went out into Farmington Avenue a little way, returning soon to deposit Jean, who at five years had to go early to bed. Then out once more until dusk. As soon as Patrick had delivered the family home again, and after Clara and Susie had been put to bed, George and Lilly Warner walked over across the grass, followed later by Annie Price [a friend of the Warners]. Lilly wandered off home after a bit, leaving Annie and George to play whist with Mark and Livy. After four games, Charles and Susan Warner came in. The company talked of Charley's most recent trip until Dr. George Williamson Smith, president of Trinity College, and a Miss Corey stopped by on their way from downtown. Since the number was now eight, two tables of whist were set up. "We had a jolly remainder of the evening," Livy winds up her diary entry, "eating ice cream, hearing and telling funny stories, of which Mr. Clemens was full."

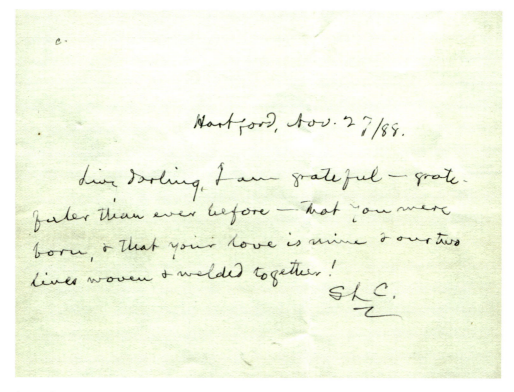

On her forty-third birthday, Sam inscribed this tribute to Livy. It was a time of prosperity and security for the family that was to wane within a few years. THE MARK TWAIN HOUSE & MUSEUM COLLECTIONS.

Thus life went on through the 1880s, as Clemens himself described it, with "servants, friends, visitors, books, dogs, cats, horses, cows, accidents, travel, joys, sorrows, lies, slanders, oppositions, persuasions, good & evil beguilements, treacheries, fidelities, the timeless & everlasting impact of character-forming exterior influences which begin their strenuous assault at our cradle & only end it at the grave."

Along with *Huckleberry Finn*, the decade produced *A Tramp Abroad*, *The Prince and the Pauper*, *Life on the Mississippi*, and *A Connecticut Yankee in King Arthur's Court*. This last was a novel drawn from his fascination with medieval life, the appeal of New England enterprise and invention, and his growing disillusionment with America's direction. His cynicism about the decline was intensified by his more politically radical illustrator, Daniel Beard, who drew a parallel between medieval monarchs, Southern slaveholders, and Gilded Age robber barons. Beard's work delighted Clemens, and the radical artist went on to help found the Boy Scouts of America. In juxtaposing medieval life and Yankee ingenuity in a time travel tale, Clemens created a volatile piece of work—funny, lyrical, and incisive, as his work always was, but with an uncharacteristically gruesome apocalyptic ending.

A Connecticut Yankee could have been an emblem for the decade. By the end of it, Clemens had gone through Livy's inheritance and much of their own family savings with his $3,000-to-$4,000-a-month typesetter investments. The machine's eighteen thousand moving parts could not function without constant breakdowns. The publishing venture, after its early success, was foundering. A financial crisis weakened the economy in 1890. By 1891, it became clear that the firm was headed for bankruptcy.

At Onteora Park, the artists' and writers' community founded by Candace Wheeler in upstate New York, the teenagers Susy and Clara Clemens peer down from their carriage at the photographer during the summer of 1890. THE MARK TWAIN HOUSE & MUSEUM. GIFT OF LAURENCE HUTTON.

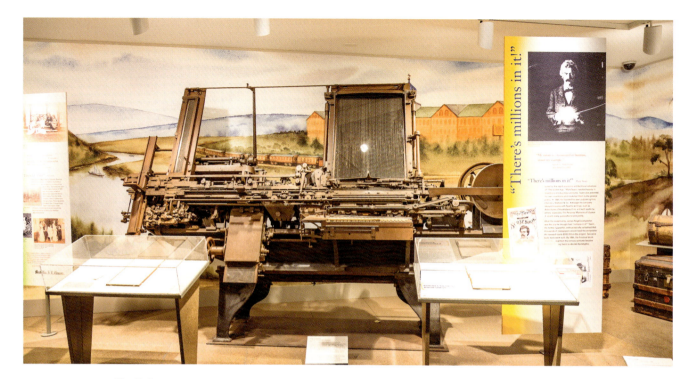

The Paige compositor, an overcomplicated, eighteen-thousand-part machine that was to replace the hand setting of printing type for all time, helped bring financial ruin to the Clemens family. The last remaining prototype of the compositor, the 1887 model, is on display in the exhibit area of the museum's Visitor Center. THE MARK TWAIN HOUSE & MUSEUM. PHOTOGRAPH BY ALANA BORGES GORDON.

Clemens halted the typesetter payments, but running the house—the equivalent of operating a small business—had become too much of a financial burden. "I wish there was some way to change our manner of living but that seems next to impossible unless we sell our house," Livy wrote. It was a physical strain, too: Livy, the manager of this household enterprise, was developing heart problems. The death of both Samuel's and Livy's mothers in 1890 had loosened their ties to America, and they chose to move to Europe, where Livy could benefit from healing baths. "The water required seems to be provided at a little obscure and little-visited nook up in the hills back of the Rhine somewhere," Clemens wrote. He could lecture and write to rebuild their finances, and life in Europe, with reasonably priced hotels and only a few servants to keep them going, would be an economy.

"We all regarded this break in a hitherto smooth flow of harmonious existence as something resembling a tragedy," Clara wrote. "We had showered love on the home itself—the library; the conservatory sweet with the perfume of flowers, the bright bedrooms. . . . We passed from room to room with leaden hearts, looked back and lingered—lingered. An inner voice whispered we should never return, and we never did."

In 1891, the year the family left the Hartford house, never to return, artist Arthur Jule Goodman made this pencil and black chalk sketch of Clemens next to the chimneypiece in the library for a magazine, *The Illustrated American*. It is the only contemporary image of the author inside the house. THE MARK TWAIN HOUSE & MUSEUM COLLECTIONS.

That was not the plan; the family hoped that after its European sojourn, they would return. But affairs with the typesetter did not improve, and the publishing company was still in trouble. The Clemenses moved from spa to spa in Europe over the coming years, with Clemens returning periodically to the United States to see to business matters, which worsened in the Panic of 1893. The typesetter failed a major test at the offices of the *Chicago Herald* late that year, and Charles L. Webster & Co. went bankrupt in 1894—Clemens's *The Tragedy of Pudd'nhead Wilson*, a tale of mistaken identity, racial confusion, and murder, was back with his old Hartford publisher, the American Publishing Company. Meanwhile, he finished a fictionalized biography of Joan of Arc, written to try to establish himself as a more serious writer, at first publishing it anonymously in installments in *Harper's* magazine.

Help from an admirer who became a friend, Henry Huttleston Rogers, a vice president of Standard Oil, was invaluable in getting Clemens's business affairs back on track, and Rogers arranged a plan for him to pay back his many debts. "The only man who is lavishing his sweat and blood to save me and mine from starvation and shame is a Standard Oil fiend," Samuel wrote Livy.

On a visit back to America in the spring of 1895, he revisited the Hartford house, now rented to Livy's old friend Alice Hooker Day and her family. Leary, the maid, had returned all the house's furnishings to their accustomed places, so the rooms looked exactly as they had when the Clemenses were there.

As soon as I entered the front door I was seized with a furious desire to have us all in this house again and right away, and never go outside the grounds any more forever. . . . And so, when I stepped in at the front door and was suddenly confronted by all its richness and beauty minus wraps and concealments, it almost took my breath away. It seemed as if I had burst awake out of a hellish dream, and had never been away, and that you would come drifting down out of those dainty upper regions with the little children tagging after you.

More hell was to come. Later that year, he embarked with Livy and Clara on a round-the-world tour with the express purpose of writing another travel book. Susy, now twenty-three, and Jean, age fifteen, remained with Livy's sister in Elmira. The Clemenses ended their voyage in England and had settled in Guildford, southwest of London, in August 1896 to await Susy and Jean's arrival, when they got word that Susy was ill.

She had been visiting friends in Hartford. When her sickness struck, Katy Leary, who had traveled to Hartford to prepare Susy for the overseas trip, moved her into the old house. There the twenty-four-year-old died of spinal meningitis on August 18. "It is one of the mysteries of our nature," Clemens wrote, "that a man, all unprepared, can receive a thunder-stroke like that and live." The family secluded themselves in deep mourning in London. In the shadow of the tragedy, birthdays and holidays, so important in the Clemens family, went unobserved. Clemens threw himself into his work.

Over the years that followed, the family still seemed poised to return to 351 Farmington Avenue. Twichell wrote to Samuel

The death of Susy Clemens in 1896 made the idea of returning to the Hartford house painful for Samuel and Livy. Three years afterward, Livy wrote to a friend, "I feel much perhaps most of the time as if I could *not* go back to Hartford. . . . I still find it very difficult to live without Susy. . . . In the old place would it not be still more nearly impossible?" THE MARK TWAIN HOUSE & MUSEUM. GIFT OF CAROLINE HARNSBERGER.

and Livy, "When are the Clemenses coming home? is a question raised hereabouts with a frequency, a tone, and an accent, which, could they be statistically and phonographically reported to you, would leave you in no doubt of the welcome that awaits your reappearance among us." But even two and a half years after Susy's death, Clemens wrote back to Twichell, "It is not the city of Hartford, it is the city of Heartbreak."

The study in Elmira was reached by a stone staircase in the hillside, and here Clemens, in one of a series of photographs taken in 1903, makes his way down toward the farmhouse owned by his sister-in-law, Susan Crane. THE MARK TWAIN HOUSE & MUSEUM. GIFT OF OLIVIA LADA-MOCARSKI.

Samuel and Livy Clemens, their Hartford house now sold, sit together on the porch at Quarry Farm in the summer of 1903. By the end of the year, the Clemenses were settled in a villa in Florence; in June 1904, Livy died there. THE MARK TWAIN HOUSE & MUSEUM. GIFT OF THE HARPERS.

In 1902, as Samuel and Livy restlessly sought to establish a new home, they put the Hartford house—by then a constant drain on their finances—on the market. It sold in 1903 for $28,800 to Richard M. Bissell, an executive who was being transferred from the Western Department of the Hartford Fire Insurance Company to the home office. Bissell arrived in the city with his wife, Marie, and their young son. If, as Clemens claimed around this time, the Clemenses had sunk as much as $110,00–$167,000 into the house since 1873, when they first stood on the Hartford hillside and planned the construction, the Bissells got a bargain.

The Clemenses' post-Hartford odyssey ended in Florence, Italy, the last of the many places Livy was brought in the hope that her health might improve. There she died on June 5, 1904. In the following years, Samuel lived in New York City and began to dictate a long, sprawling autobiography. Finally, his financial footing firmly grounded, he built another Connecticut house—not at all like the first, but an Italianate villa on top of a hill in Redding, sixty miles west of Hartford. There, Clara, who was embarking on a career as a concert singer, married the pianist and conductor Ossip Gabrilowitsch in October 1909.

Two months later came another family tragedy. Jean, now twenty-nine years old, had begun suffering epileptic seizures when she was a teenager. She had undergone various treatments and was sheltered from excitements—including relationships with men—that were then believed to aggravate the condition. Rules based on these attitudes largely kept her apart from her family, though some scholars believe it was pressure from Clemens's secretary, Isabel Lyon, that added to this separation. Clemens broke dramatically with Lyon, and Jean

In his final years, his fortunes restored, Clemens had a house built in Redding, a small rural town in western Connecticut. The house, called Stormfield, was designed by the son of his editor and friend, William Dean Howells, in an Italianate style far different from that of the Hartford house. THE MARK TWAIN HOUSE & MUSEUM COLLECTIONS.

In October 1909, Clemens's daughter Clara married pianist and conductor Ossip Gabrilowitsch at Stormfield. Left to right are Clemens, in the cap and gown he had worn in England to receive an honorary degree at the University of Oxford in 1907; nephew Jervis Langdon; daughter Jean Clemens; Ossip Gabrilowitsch; Clara Clemens; and Reverend Joseph Twichell, Clemens's old friend, who performed the service. THE MARK TWAIN HOUSE & MUSEUM COLLECTIONS.

finally joined her father at Redding in early 1909 to work as his secretary. There she formed a local group against cruelty to animals, helped with the local lending library her father had founded, carved intricate wooden chests, and rode her horse through the Connecticut countryside. After decorating the house for Christmas Eve, she suffered a seizure and died of a heart attack. Clemens, too ill to go to the funeral, titled the last, poignant section of his autobiography "The Death of Jean."

Jean Clemens was an equestrian, wood carver, and advocate for animal rights during her brief life. She was separated from her father for years on the theory that, as a person with epilepsy, she needed complete rest in sanitariums. She was finally restored to the house in Redding, where she took over management of the household. On Christmas Eve 1909, she died suddenly of heart failure during a seizure. THE MARK TWAIN HOUSE & MUSEUM. GIFT OF OLIVIA LADA-MOCARSKI.

Before being taken to his final resting place in Elmira, Clemens was honored in a twenty-minute service at the Brick Church at Fifth Avenue and Thirty-Seventh Street in New York. Friends and fellow writers saw him off before his coffin was carried to the waiting horse-drawn hearse.
THE MARK TWAIN HOUSE & MUSEUM COLLECTIONS.

When Clemens himself died four months later, his friend Twichell wrote of him, "With all his brilliant prosperities he had lived to be a lonely, weary-hearted man, and the thought of his departure hence was not unwelcome to him."

CHAPTER EIGHT
"I Knew Mark Twain"

IN HARTFORD, THE BISSELLS HAD SETTLED INTO their new home; another son and daughter were born while they lived there. Richard Bissell, who began a twenty-eight-year tenure as president of the Hartford Fire Insurance Company around this time, was "tall, distinguished looking, quietly confident and able," as a company history has said. He was, however, described by a son as "a somewhat distant figure at home."

His wife Marie was another matter altogether. Raised in Minnesota, she was "a midwesterner who found Hartford society stuffy," says historian Eugene R. Gaddis. "Even during Prohibition, champagne flowed liberally at her soirées, and on the morning after at least one party, a grand piano was spotted on her front lawn." She later became a patron of the legendary director of the Wadsworth Atheneum art museum, A. Everett "Chick" Austin, who in the 1930s brought the likes of Gertrude Stein, Piet Mondrian, and George Balanchine to Hartford. Marie Bissell once appeared onstage with Austin in a black satin riding outfit designed by Pavel Tchelitchew, the Russian surrealist painter.

The Bissells' son, Richard Bissell Jr., remembered that his brother kept a pet alligator in the Clemenses' conservatory and that his mother "updated the interior [of the house] to eliminate its Victorian darkness." The Tiffany stenciling in the drawing room, woefully out of date, was covered with fashionable, light-colored grass cloth paper; other stenciled walls were painted over. But the general form of the house could not be altered. "With queer little balconies and curiously shaped closets under the eaves, the house was a world unto itself," the younger Richard Bissell remembered.

The Bissells founded a nursery school for their children and their friends in the billiard room that grew into a school for boys. When the Bissells moved to suburban Farmington, they leased the house to what by then was called Kingswood School. Photographs of the era show baseball teams posed on

The family that bought the house from the Clemenses included Marie Bissell, a Midwesterner who held fabulous parties and later worked with famed modernist curator Chick Austin at Hartford's Wadsworth Atheneum art museum. Here, in the conservatory, she holds her youngest, Richard, while daughter Anne-Caroline and son William (who kept a pet alligator in the glass structure) snuggle up to her. THE MARK TWAIN HOUSE & MUSEUM COLLECTIONS.

the hillside below the house, its decorated brick and conservatory clearly visible in the background. The library became an assembly hall, the drawing room a library, the carriage house a gymnasium, and the mahogany room the headmaster's apartment.

When Kingswood School occupied the Mark Twain House in the late 1910s and early 1920s, the baseball team posed on the slope behind the house. THE MARK TWAIN HOUSE & MUSEUM COLLECTIONS.

In 1920, the Bissells sold the property to a real estate investor, J. J. Wall, and two brothers in the undertaking business, John and Francis Ahern, for $55,000. Two months later, a notice appeared in the *Hartford Courant* announcing that the new owners proposed to raze it and build an apartment building.

A group called the Artist's Club of Hartford protested, meeting in the studio of a local landscape painter named Nunzio Vayana to plot strategy for preserving the building. They planned "a campaign which will embrace all parts of the country where there resides one admirer of Mark Twain" and rounded up support from celebrities ranging from President Woodrow Wilson to the tenor Enrico Caruso. The energetic young editor of the *Courant*, Emile Gauvreau, urged the publisher to get on the bandwagon.

The publisher, however, was Charles Hopkins Clark, who had been editor of the solidly Republican paper in 1884—the year that Clemens, in his billiard room, had heard the news via George Griffin of the nomination of the corrupt James G. Blaine and resolved to stand with Cleveland and his conscience rather than with his party. Almost forty years later, Clark still resented this betrayal.

"I knew Mark Twain," Clark told Gauvreau. "When he came to Hartford he gave everybody the idea that he was a Republican. I think he must have been a Democrat all the time. He and his crony, Holy Joe Twichell, voted for Cleveland after we had come out for Blaine . . . Mark Twain spent all his time laughing at people and finally he had to move out of here." The city editor, Harry Horton, said simply, "Hartford never liked Mark Twain."

The Artist's Club pressed on. Wall offered to sell the house to the group for $300,000, almost six times what he and the Aherns had paid for it. If they didn't want to buy, he said, he would "take off that ugly roof" and add three stories to the house. Even Clark, nursing his 1884 Blaine resentments, couldn't resist the tide of protest this statement raised. The *Courant* condemned the speculators, and the Republican governor of the state, Marcus Holcomb, added his voice in support of preservation. Pennies were collected from schoolchildren, a tea dance was organized on the *ombra*, and a young woman dressed as Joan of Arc was to appear on horseback, the whole to be filmed by the artist Vayana. A Mark Twain Memorial Association was incorporated.

Then, surprisingly, the whole effort dissipated. Perhaps it was because the owners became a little more public relations conscious. They neither tore down the house nor destroyed the elaborately patterned roof of multicolored slate, instead simply converting the rooms into apartments "with composition board partitions in the larger rooms." They noted that the walls could be easily removed "in the event of its being desired to restore the interior to its original condition or as a memorial to Mark Twain." In 1925, Wall and the Aherns sold the house to new owners for $82,500.

That same year, a woman with impeccable Nook Farm lineage visited friends in the Adirondacks in New York State and laid out her own vision for the Mark Twain House—and for the Harriet Beecher Stowe house nearby. Katharine Seymour Day was the daughter of Livy's friend, Alice Hooker Day.

Katharine Seymour Day had a vision of a literary center uniting the great writers of Nook Farm: her great-aunt, Harriet Beecher Stowe; Samuel Clemens; and Charles Dudley Warner, not much regarded today but known for his collaboration with Clemens on *The Gilded Age*. COURTESY OF THE HARRIET BEECHER STOWE CENTER.

The Days has rented the Clemens home while Samuel and Livy were in Europe in the 1890s, and it was for them that Katy Leary had uncovered and set out the furnishings in March 1895. This was the time when Clemens returned for a visit and was overcome with nostalgia, wishing the whole family back in the house for good.

Day had quarts of Beecher blood—her grandmother was Isabella Beecher Hooker and her great-aunt Harriet Beecher Stowe. The old Nook Farm was dispersed and gone, but Day had an idea for the future. She was a person who had lived her life in a perpetual state of education, studying painting in Paris and New York and in her forties studying psychology, philosophy, and anthropology at Radcliffe, Columbia, and Berkeley.

She told her Adirondack neighbors of her vision for a literary center based on the two writers' houses so close to each other—and then wrote her mother, now seventy-seven years old, that her fellow mountain vacationers approved "my plan for the Stowe house" and her concern for "the state of the Clemens one." She said she pictured a Nook Farm library for research on the Beechers and their neighbors.

Back in Hartford, she pitched into Farmington Avenue zoning battles, challenging the increasing commercialization of the neighborhood, and formed a group called the Friends of Hartford to lobby the city government—"the local Tammany," she called them—and pursue her project. The Stowe house and the Potter-designed home where George and Lilly Warner had lived were fairly safe, she thought, as those living in them had family connections to the original occupants. (The Warner house had also been the home of George's brother Charles Dudley Warner, adding another literary connection to Day's mission.) But the acquisition of the Clemens house "is the key," she told the Chamber of Commerce. She had bigger ideas, and better connections, than the Artist's Club. She also had a Joan of Arc to present—but this time it was a stage production at Parson's Theater on Prospect Street downtown, and the leading lady was Clara Clemens Gabrilowitsch herself. A campaign was set up to raise the money to purchase the house and refurbish it.

Charles Hopkins Clark had passed on, but there were still those who whispered against the plan, saying the house was an "architectural monstrosity." Finally, the mayor of Hartford stepped in, issuing a proclamation that the people of Hartford should consider it a "duty" to contribute to the effort. On April 29, 1929, the General Assembly of the State of Connecticut issued a charter to the Mark Twain Memorial and Library Commission. There was a final push

In April 1930, Clara Clemens Gabrilowitsch and her husband Ossip attended a reception opening the new library in her childhood home. A *Hartford Courant* clipping was carefully marked to identify some of the participants, standing in a row in front of the house's porch. Clara and Ossip are fourth and fifth from the left; at center, in a light dress, is Katharine Seymour Day, whose active efforts helped save the house. THE MARK TWAIN HOUSE & MUSEUM COLLECTIONS.

for funds and even a donation from the landowners that effectively reduced the price of the house to $150,000, with a mortgage of $55,000. To help pay the mortgage, the Hartford Public Library would rent the ground floor, and the Mark Twain Memorial would continue to rent apartments on the upper floors. A reception was attended by Clara and Ossip Gabrilowitsch, who had given a joint recital the night before to raise funds. The house, Clara said charitably, "now really looks like my own former home, the scene of my childhood days."

The house even had one of her childhood friends in it; a Miss Helen Forrest moved into what Clara and Susy had considered the "spooky" guest room on the third floor and used the billiard room as a living room. An official of the Memorial reported to Clara that Forrest was "just as happy as she can be to live in the home where so many of her happiest days of childhood were spent as guests of the family she adored and still does for that matter."

Despite the income from such tenants and the public library branch, the hard times of the Depression increased the house's debt. Even a fundraising speech by Winston Churchill in 1932—Clemens had introduced Churchill at a meeting in New York's Waldorf Astoria in 1900—cleared the Memorial only $350.70.

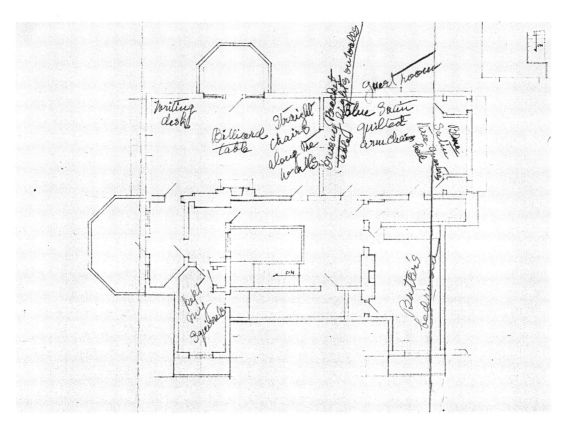

In the 1950s, daughter Clara, by then Clara Samossoud, helped the initial restoration effort with advice and memories of life in the house more than sixty years before. In 1957, she was asked to put her memory to work writing the location of various items of furniture and other features of the house on a plan showing the various rooms. She clearly located her father's writing table in the corner of the billiard room, as well as the furnishings of the adjacent Artist's Friend's room. She also noted a room where she and Susy had kept their pet squirrels. THE MARK TWAIN HOUSE & MUSEUM COLLECTIONS.

The centennial of Mark Twain's birth in 1935 was celebrated in a relatively low-budget way. During World War II, with coal needed to power defense plants, the thermostats in the vast, chilly building had to be locked up to prevent tenants from trying to squeeze a little more heat into the radiators. In the meadow downhill, where the Clemenses' cows had grazed, a Victory Garden grew.

A 1947 mystery novel, *Murder Stalks the Circle* by Lee Thayer, provides a snapshot of apartment life in the house. Private eye Peter Clancy lives in a third-floor apartment in the Mark Twain House with his "perfect valet," Wiggar. One rainy night, he catches a taxi ride home from the theater: Wiggar is at the curb, ready with an umbrella, and the two make a dash to the porch.

> *Only a dim light burned in the square entrance hall, showing the closed doors of the branch library that occupied the spacious old living rooms. The heavy red-velvet-covered rope that blocked the wide staircase during borrowing hours was now hooked in a loop*

against the wall, giving tenants free access to the half dozen apartments above . . . Wiggar restored the catch on the heavy front door, making sure that it was fast, and followed his master up the broad walnut-paneled staircase to the top of the house.

The door to what had once been a billiard room was partly open and a cheerful bright light streamed across the hall, but it did little to alleviate the gloom of the deep square well of the staircase, though there was one bulb burning on each landing.

In the 1950s, Katharine Day, after decades of pioneering stewardship, resigned as president of the Memorial, and a new generation emerged. Edith Colgate Salsbury became a trustee and immediately began a level of activity that Walter K. Schwinn, the 1980s historian of the house, described:

> *After joining the Board she appeared almost daily at the house, arriving with a basket that carried her noontime lunch and her agenda for the day. She performed almost every task that needed to be done—drafting plans, raising funds, soliciting memberships, arranging benefits, devising publicity, carrying out research and, when the need arose, whitewashing the walls and sweeping the floors.*

Director Edith Salsbury and others got the restoration effort moving in the 1950s. In this 1965 photo, she unveils her engaging account of life in the Clemens household taken from the actual words of family members and others, *Susy and Mark Twain*. With her are Norman Holmes Pearson, who added scholarly weight to the effort, and Walter Schwinn, who later wrote an important history of the Mark Twain House.
THE MARK TWAIN HOUSE & MUSEUM COLLECTIONS.

Robert Schutz, another active member, was the grandson of the Clemens's homeopathic physician, Dr. Cincinnatus Taft. Atwood Collins II was a lawyer with deep roots in Hartford; his grandfather had invited Clemens's friend Twichell to preside over Asylum Hill Congregational Church. There were many others, with essential skills in architecture, literature, and—perhaps most important at the time—raising funds from foundations and corporations. Professionalism was taking the organization out of the era when visitors were charged a dime to take a look at Mark Twain's bed (which Clara had given to the Memorial in 1940). They adopted a plan setting out five objectives, stressing the development of the house as a literary center, a house restoration, a museum, a library, and a location for lectures and classes.

And on May 18, 1956, a young man who had made a name for himself doing a stage representation of Mark Twain said he'd perform for free at the Memorial's annual meeting—Hal Holbrook, embarking on his masterful, multi-decade career bringing Clemens alive for those living a century past his lifetime.

Hal Holbrook first performed for the benefit of the Mark Twain House in 1956. In 1960, he put on his makeup for a performance in the library. There were decades of visits and support to follow from the man who brought Samuel Clemens, a modern man in his time, into the twenty-first century.
THE MARK TWAIN HOUSE & MUSEUM COLLECTIONS.

The house's mortgage was paid off in 1959, and the years that followed saw a renewed push toward repair, first, and then meticulous restoration. A visitor during this era found the staff "proud, chatty, and dedicated." Documentary research was supplemented by interviews with those who still remembered the house in its heyday. And there were marvels of restoration and retrieval, hours and hours of uncompensated work supplemented by the occasional spark of

Walter K. Schwinn, president of the Memorial from 1965 to 1970 and the author of a detailed but unpublished history of the house, shows Hal Holbrook some of the restoration work in the 1960s.
THE MARK TWAIN HOUSE & MUSEUM COLLECTIONS.

pure luck. Reading of it in a Memorial newsletter in 1860, Clara (now Clara Clemens Sammosoud) praised "the *generous* people who are turning the Hartford house into a fairy-tale success of its old-time charm. . . . My Mother and Father must *feel* what is being done. I am sure that they do."

There was the great Scottish chimneypiece in the library, for instance, that had come from Ayton Castle. The Clemenses had it removed and put in storage when they sold the house in 1903. When Clemens built his house in Redding four years later, he had the mantel section installed around a fireplace. The Redding house, with new owners after Clemens's death, burned in 1923, and, according to Schwinn, "the general assumption was that the mantel was destroyed with it." He continued: "That this was not the case was revealed when in the course of a tour in 1958 [actually 1957], a guide described the mantel and its presumed fate. After hearing the description a visitor spoke up, expressing the opinion that the mantel and overmantel were in fact stored in his father's barn in Redding."

It seems the new owners had remodeled the mantel, preferring something more modern, and the chimneypiece had been stored in pieces nearby when the Redding house burned. A purchase was arranged, and the mantel returned to its place during the Clemens tenancy.

In 1963, the house was placed on the Register of National Historic Landmarks. The Tiffany stenciling in the front hall was reproduced by skilled craftsmen in that decade. A restored billiard room was dedicated in 1969. In September 1974, one hundred years after the Clemenses arrived in the upstairs rooms, while the carpenters continued their work below, the Mark Twain House was opened to the public in its restored glory with a citywide celebration.

This time, the carpenters—and the decorators, and the roofers, and the historical restoration specialists, and the HVAC engineers—have never left. With successive directors, curators, and experts in the wings, work has gone on, details have been revised and re-revised: More stenciling, for example, went on in the 1970s, and then a good deal of it was redone in the early 2000s in line with updated research. The exterior and roof got an extensive makeover in the 1990s, and the billiard room was overhauled. Revised views of the house's history brought revisions in the house itself. Clemens's telephone, for example, was believed for decades to have been in a closet off the entry hall—guides would switch on a recording of the actual voice of Hal Holbrook booming from it—and then determined to have been in the kitchen, to which it was moved.

A major development in the late 1990s was the decision to build a visitor center for what had now changed its name from the Mark Twain Memorial to The Mark Twain House & Museum. The $19 million building, designed by Robert A. M. Stern—set into a hillside to keep its profile low in relation to the Mark Twain House itself—added needed exhibit space, an auditorium, a classroom, a shop, a café, and other facilities. The ambition involved in this building project, along with an economic downturn, brought the museum to a financial low

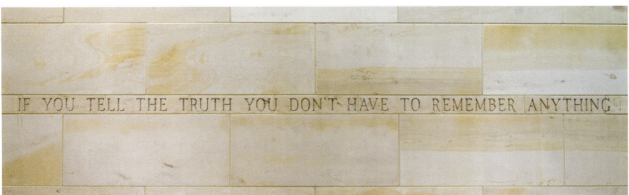

The Visitor Center, which nestles in a hillside behind the house so as not to overwhelm the view, was designed by Robert A. M. Stern and opened in 2003. It includes the vast Hal Holbrook Hall, a theater, display space for both permanent and temporary exhibitions, classrooms, a gift shop, and a café. Mark Twain quotations are incised in the interior walls of the building, providing wise and witty advice for visitors to file away. THE MARK TWAIN HOUSE & MUSEUM. PHOTOGRAPHS BY JOHN GROO.

in 2008. But donors came out of the woodwork with funds and in-kind work of all types to keep the place afloat. By 2010, the centennial of Mark's death, the museum was back on an even financial keel. Shortly afterward, The Mark Twain House & Museum was added to the Connecticut Freedom Trail, which connects places important to African American history in the state. The designation honors Clemens's actions—in *Adventures of Huckleberry Finn*, "The United States of Lyncherdom," his anti-imperialist writings, and elsewhere—furthering racial equality.

In the years since, the museum has embarked on a new level of activity ranging from lectures and scholarly conclaves, both virtual and in person, to ghost tours—spooky events with redeeming educational value, of course. There is the lively Living History program, the one that provides tours led by "Livy Clemens" and other members of the household.

Before those events, however, there had been another major restoration. The Mark Twain House had always been described as a nineteen-room mansion—but in fact there were twenty-five rooms. No one had ever counted the rooms in the semi-detached kitchen wing, the base for the servants' numerous activities, as being part of the show. The lives of the servants had been alluded to in tours of the house, and tales of Griffin and Leary were often repeated, but the "building archaeology" that went on in 2003–2004 and the restoration that followed brought a whole new dimension to the visitor experience.

The Irish Americans, African Americans, and German Americans—all those young women and men who went into service in nineteenth-century Hartford—provided the foundation on which the Clemens family was able to live the happy and sociable life they had here. It was to these people the Clemenses owed the fact that they could take a carriage ride on a summer evening, or awaken to fires lit in the grate, or sit down to a full, elegantly plated meal in the dining room, or retire to the billiard room to scrawl out three thousand words of wit and energy each day at a plain pedestal table.

Clara, when little, got it right, adding the names of a cloud of servants to her own when introduced to strangers: "Clara Lewis O'Day Botheker McAleer McLaughlin Clemens." Mark Twain's house, owned and paid for and managed by his extraordinary wife, was supported by these named and unnamed servants. And there were those who, as Samuel Clemens said, "tarried a while, were dissatisfied with us or we with them, & presently vanished out of our life." Learning of these lives "peoples and embellishes" this house, just as Edward Tuckerman Potter did for Mary Mason Fairbanks all those years ago.

Backstage at a Bewitching Place

SINCE ITS INCORPORATION IN 1929, The Mark Twain House & Museum has accumulated an important collection of books, manuscripts, photographs, and furnishings, both on display in the house and in storage. The following items are among many that were owned by the Clemens family and are cared for by the museum.

All photographs in this chapter were taken by Alana Borges Gordon.

THE SWAPPED HIGH HAT

Among the museum's holdings is this silk high hat, which provided Samuel Clemens and a priest with a chance to exchange jokes. The author was in London with his family in 1899, and after a luncheon party at a club, he went to pick up his hat in the checkroom. There was only one hat left, and it was not his. It fit him perfectly, though, and he determined from initials inside that it belonged to Basil Wilberforce, a prominent Anglican priest who was the canon (or administrator) of Westminster Abbey. He wrote to Wilberforce:

> *During the past four hours I have not been able to take anything that did not belong to me; during all that time I have not been able to stretch a fact beyond the frontiers of truth try as I might, & meantime, not only my morals have moved the astonishment of all who have come in contact with me, but my manners have gained more compliments than they have been accustomed to. This mystery is causing my family much alarm.*

Not to be outdone, Wilberforce wrote back:

> *I have been conscious of a vivacity and facility of expression this afternoon beyond the normal and I have just discovered the reason!! I have seen the historic signature "Mark Twain" in my hat!!*

In 1933, Clemens's friend and official biographer, Albert Bigelow Paine, donated the hat—Clemens's, that is—that was the subject of this tale, signature and all, to the Mark Twain Memorial, now The Mark Twain House & Museum.

The Mark Twain House & Museum, 1933.1. Gift of Albert Bigelow Paine.

COSTLY CUFF LINKS

This pair of topaz cuff links belonged to Samuel Clemens and is in its original box from the jeweler Dwight Buell of Hartford. Buell's shop was on Main Street near the city's Old State House. Samuel and Livy Clemens bought items there, and Buell was a family friend. It was Buell who, in 1881, suggested to Samuel that he invest in a mechanical typesetter being developed by James Paige—an investment that led to financial disaster for the Clemenses, as described in chapter 7.

Buell worked as a silversmith and watchmaker starting in 1852, when he was nineteen, and was a prominent and respected local citizen by the 1880s. He died in February 1889 when a boiler explosion in the Park Central Hotel, where he lived, leveled the building. Twenty-one others died on what Clemens's friend Reverend Twichell called "a dark and terrible day for Hartford." Buell's obituary said that his business "has been conducted by him in a very successful manner, making hosts of friends, who felt that his word could always be depended upon" and noted his "kindly disposition and never-failing geniality."

The Mark Twain House & Museum, 2013.22.1a-c. Gift of Colonel and Mrs. James E. Townes Jr.

A SLEIGH FIT FOR A QUEEN

This sleigh was used by Samuel Clemens in his final home in Redding, Connecticut, where he lived from 1907 until his death in 1910. It was pulled by a white horse named Sami Ramus (probably a variant of Semiramus, a legendary queen of Babylon), according to Pierpont Adams of Redding, who gave the sleigh to the Mark Twain Memorial in 1958. As Adams told it, Clemens had presented the sleigh to Adams's stepfather, Judge Samuel Shaw. (Another version of the story mentions a slightly different ownership trail.) Adams said Clemens's coachman, George O'Connor, would meet Shaw at the station in Georgetown, Connecticut, with a buffalo robe to keep the judge warm and a box of hot oats to help the horse retain heat.

A December 1908 *New York Times* story told how Clemens's daughter Clara and her future husband, the Russian pianist Ossip Gabrilowitch, went for a sleigh ride in Redding. The horse was frightened by "a wind-whipped newspaper" and bolted.

> *Mr. Gabrilowitsch, who was driving, lost control of the horse. At the top of a hill the sleigh overturned, and Miss Clemens was thrown out. At the right of the summit of the hill is a drop of fifty feet. When the sleigh turned over the Russian leaped to the ground, and caught the horse by the head, stopping it as it was about to plunge over the bank, dragging Miss Clemens, whose dress had caught in the runner.*
>
> *In leaping to rescue Miss Clemens he sprained his right ankle. Miss Clemens was picked up uninjured, but suffered greatly from the shock of the accident. The injury to the pianist's ankle was painful, but he helped Miss Clemens into the sleigh, and drove her to her home.*

The Mark Twain House & Museum, 1958.107. Gift of Pierpont Adams.

BILLIARD BALLS SPARK A FRIENDSHIP

"The game of billiards has destroyed my naturally sweet disposition," Clemens said with his customary straight face in a 1906 speech. He started playing the game in his youth but really took to it in his twenties when he worked as a miner, political functionary, and journalist in the West from 1861 to 1867. During the years he spent in Hartford, long and late-night games with a group of friends—like the one that led to his political revolt from the Republican Party, described in the "Billiard Room" section of chapter 4—were routine.

After the family left the Hartford house in 1891, opportunities for billiards were fewer, but the gift of the table now in the billiard room in 1906 brought him back to the game with a vengeance. His official biographer, Albert Bigelow Paine, credited this table with bringing the two men together as friends, and they played together constantly.

Paine's grandson Bigelow Paine Cushman (and his wife, Anne Cushman) donated these balls to the Mark Twain Memorial in 1968. They are made of ivory; four or five could be made from a single elephant's tusk. (Today's billiard balls are made from a type of resin.)

The Mark Twain House & Museum, 1968.6.1, 1968.6.2, 1968.6.4. Gifts of Mr. and Mrs. Bigelow Cushman.

KEEPSAKES FOR ELLEN O'NEIL

John O'Neil and his wife, Ellen, emigrated from Ireland in 1871 and joined the Clemens family in Hartford in 1885, when John was hired as gardener. After the Clemenses left for Europe in 1891, the O'Neils moved into the house as caretakers. The following year, Livy wrote to Ellen O'Neil, "I am sure everything is going well and I do not have one single moment of worry about anything there. I know that you and John will take good care of everything." In the early 1900s, the O'Neils supplemented the $70 a month the Clemenses provided by selling perennials from the greenhouse on the property.

When the house was sold in 1903, Livy let the O'Neils keep several items of furniture—and gave Ellen this MacKinnon stylographic pen with its case and filling bulb, enamel-topped inkwell, and pen wipe. The Mark Twain Memorial purchased the items from a descendant in 1973.

The Mark Twain House & Museum, 1959.37.3 A-C.

A FLORENTINE SHIRT

The Clemenses lived in Florence, Italy, on two separate occasions The first was in 1892–1893, when Clemens described the villa they rented as

> *three miles from Florence, on the side of a hill. . . . To see the sun sink down, drowned on his pink and purple and golden floods, and overwhelm Florence with tides of color that make all the sharp lines dim and faint and turn the solid city to a city of dreams, is a sight to stir the coldest nature and make a sympathetic one drunk with ecstasy.*

Their second stay was a sadder one. They had returned hoping that the Italian climate would help restore Livy, suffering from cardiac disease, to health, but she died there on June 5, 1904.

On one of these stays, Clemens probably purchased this cotton dress shirt with an intricately intertwined "SLC" monogram (hand embroidered in red thread) and mother-of-pearl buttons. The maker's label reads "A Dalmasso/Florence/Tomabuoni 17." (Tomabuoni is a Florence street still dotted with high-end clothing boutiques; number 17 is now home to a fashion school.) The shirt passed from the Clemenses' lady's maid, Katy Leary, to a friend, and from her to a nephew, whose wife sold the shirt to the museum.

The Mark Twain House & Museum, 1964.23.001.

WOODCARVING AS THERAPY

As noted, Jean Clemens's history of seizures and confinement, from which she was freed only shortly before her death at twenty-nine, is one of the most poignant stories of the Clemens family. Her spirit shone throughout her short life in her love of animals and activism against their mistreatment, her passion for horse riding and other outdoor sports, and her woodcarving. She started carving lessons in 1897. In later life she would hire carpenters to make boxes and bookracks and then draw and carve elaborate designs on them. It took her fifteen hours to make a bookrack, she estimated, and worried all the time that her concentration might bring on a seizure.

Among the Mark Twain House's collections are her woodcarving tools and creations that include the glove box shown here, with its intertwined foliate and scroll decoration. The initials "JLC"—her full name was Jane Lampton Clemens—are carved on the lid, and the year "1900" on the front face.

The Mark Twain House & Museum, 1987.10.1.

CLARA'S WATCH

Henry Capt was a famed Geneva watchmaker whose timekeeping devices sometimes included buttons that set off music or hidden automata—moving metal figures dancing, playing the harp, or even indulging in erotic situations. He was active in the early 1800s, and his work was much in demand throughout the century. This watch, which Clara Clemens owned, was a simple "open face style" pocket watch that attached to her clothing with a pin.

The watch has a white porcelain dial with green enamel numerals and a green enamel back case with diamonds set in a foliate motif. The inside is engraved "Clara Langdon Clemens/June 8th 1892." The date is Clara's eighteenth birthday, when she was in Berlin with her family, preparing to study piano there. The watch can be seen pinned to Clara's dress in a photograph taken with her parents during the 1895–1896 around-the-world lecture tour that resulted in Clemens's travel book *Following the Equator*.

The Mark Twain House & Museum, 2007.3.1. Gift of Johannette Rowley, in loving memory of Mildred T. Centuio.

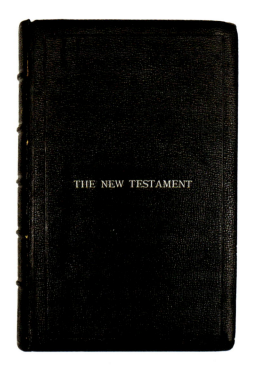
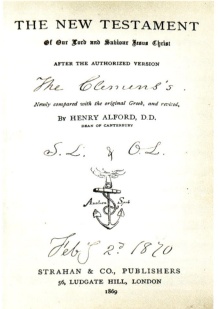

A SIGNIFICANT MARRIAGE

On February 2, 1870, this copy of the New Testament was used by Reverend Thomas K. Beecher of Elmira and Reverend Joseph Twichell of Hartford to marry Samuel and Olivia Clemens in the parlor of Olivia's childhood home. A few days after their wedding, Clemens wrote to his friend William Bowen, gushing over his new bride:

> I have at this moment the only sweetheart I ever loved, & bless her old heart she is lying asleep upstairs in a bed that I sleep in every night, & for four whole days she has been Mrs. Samuel L. Clemens! I am 34 & she is 24; I am young & very handsome (I make the statement with the fullest confidence, for I got it from her,) & she is much the most beautiful girl I ever saw (I said that before she was anything to me, & so it is worthy of all belief).

The Mark Twain House Museum, 4296.97.3.

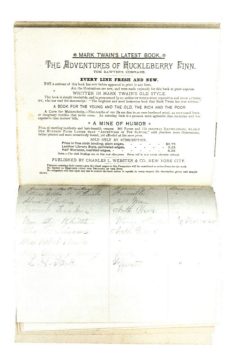
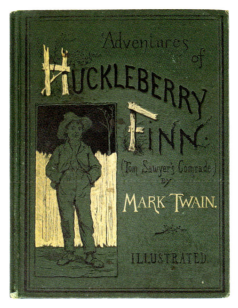

PROSPECTUS FOR A CLASSIC

Samuel Clemens's first bestseller writing as Mark Twain was *The Innocents Abroad: Or, the New Pilgrim's Progress*, published in 1869 by the American Publishing Company of Hartford. Its success sold Clemens on the publisher's system of selling books by subscription—that is, by employing door-to-door salespeople to sell customers books, rather than distributing them through bookstores. As a visual aid for sale of a book, a publisher produced a bound prospectus that included sample chapters, sample bindings, the table of contents, and sample illustrations. Subscription books would go for a premium price, but after an initial surge of sales, cheaper copies would be "dumped" into bookstores, sometimes specifically timed for holiday buying.

When Clemens started his own publishing company—Charles L. Webster & Co. (named for his nephew and partner)—in 1884, he used the same system. This prospectus for his company's first book, *Adventures of Huckleberry Finn*, was not without its pitfalls, however. After 3,000 copies of the prospectus had been printed and at least 250 shipped to salespeople around the country, an agent in Chicago noticed that one of the illustrations had been altered in an obscene way. The illustration was hastily withdrawn—an agent who didn't tear it out of his or her prospectus and return it would be fired on the spot—and corrected copies were printed and distributed. The museum's copy shown here is one of the corrected versions.

The Mark Twain House & Museum, 753.72. Gift of Jonathan Goodwin.

Bibliography

The central clearinghouse for letters to and from the Clemens family is the Mark Twain Papers and Project at the University of California, Berkeley. The Project's comprehensive list of letters to and from Twain, sorted by recipient or by proper name keyword and indicating the present location of the letter if not in the Project's own substantial collection, is available on the Project website, lib.berkeley.edu/visit/bancroft/mark-twain-papers. All quoted letters are from *Microfilm Edition of Mark Twain's Manuscript Letters Now in the Mark Twain Papers*, 11 vols. (Berkeley: Bancroft Library, 2001), and *Microfilm Edition of Mark Twain's Previously Unpublished Letters*, 8 vols. (Berkeley: Bancroft Library, 2001).

Aldrich, Mrs. Thomas Bailey. *Crowding Memories*. Boston, MA, and New York: Houghton Mifflin, 1920.

Andrews, Gregory E., and David F. Ransom. *Structures and Styles: Guided Tours of Hartford Architecture*. Hartford: Connecticut Historical Society and Connecticut Architecture Foundation, 1988.

Andrews, Kenneth R. *Nook Farm: Mark Twain's Hartford Circle*. Cambridge, MA: Harvard University Press, 1950.

Baldwin, Peter. *Domesticating the Street: The Reform of Public Space in Hartford, 1850–1930*. Columbus: Ohio State University Press, 1999.

Bissell, Richard. *My Life on the Mississippi: Or Why I Am Not Mark Twain*. Boston and Toronto: Little, Brown & Co., 1973.

Bissell, Richard M., Jr. *Reflections of a Cold Warrior: From Yalta to the Bay of Pigs*. New Haven, CT, and London: Yale University Press, 1996.

Brooks, Van Wyck. *The Ordeal of Mark Twain*. New York: E. P. Dutton, 1920.

Bush, Harold K., Steve Courtney, and Peter Messent, eds. *The Letters of Mark Twain and Joseph Hopkins Twichell*. Athens: University of Georgia Press, 2017.

Bush, Robert. "Grace King and Mark Twain." Unpublished manuscript in The Mark Twain House & Museum Archive, n.d.

Chafee, Richard. "Edward Tuckerman Potter and Samuel Clemens: An Architect and His Client." Unpublished MA thesis, Yale University, 1966.

Clark, Charles Hopkins. "The Charter Oak City." *Scribner's Monthly*, November 1876.

Clemens, Clara. *My Father, Mark Twain*. New York: Harper & Brothers, 1931.

Clemens, Samuel L. *Autobiography of Mark Twain*, vols. 1–3. Edited by Harriet Elinor Smith and other editors of the Mark Twain Project. Berkeley: University of California Press, 2010, 2013, and 2015.

——. *A Connecticut Yankee in King Arthur's Court*. New York: Charles L. Webster & Co., 1889.

——. *A Family Sketch and Other Private Writings*. Edited by Benjamin Griffin. Berkeley: University of California Press, 2014.

——. "Jane Lampton Clemens." In *Mark Twain's Hannibal, Huck & Tom*. Edited by Walter Blair. Berkeley: University of California Press, 1969.

——. *Life on the Mississippi*. Boston: James R. Osgood & Co., 1883.

——. *Mark Twain's Letters*, vol. 5, *1872–1873*. Edited by Lin Salamo and Harriet Elinor Smith. Berkeley: University of California Press, 1997.

——. *Mark Twain's Letters*, vol. 6, *1874–1875*. Edited by Michael B. Frank and Harriet Elinor Smith. Berkeley: University of California Press, 2002.

——. *Mark Twain's Notebooks and Journals*, vols. 1–3. Berkeley: University of California Press, 1975 and 1979.

——. *Roughing It*. Hartford, CT: American Publishing Co., 1880.

——. *A Tramp Abroad*. Hartford, CT: American Publishing Co., 1872.

Courtney, Steve. *Joseph Hopkins Twichell: The Life and Times of Mark Twain's Closest Friend*. Athens: University of Georgia Press, 2008.

Daniel, Hawthorne. *The Hartford of Hartford: An Insurance Company's Part in a Century and a Half of American History*. New York: Random House, 1960.

DeVoto, Bernard. *Mark Twain's America*. Lincoln: University of Nebraska Press, 1932.

Driscoll, Kerry. "Mark Twain's Music Box: Livy, Cosmopolitanism, and the Commodity Aesthetic." In *Cosmopolitan Twain*, edited by Anne M. Ryan and Joseph B. McCullough, 140–86. Columbia, MO, and London: University of Missouri Press, 2008.

Faude, Wilson H. "Associated Artists and the American Renaissance in the Decorative Arts." *Winterthur Portfolio* 10 (1975): 101–30.

——. *The Renaissance of Mark Twain's House: Handbook for Restoration*. Larchmont, NY: Queens House, 1978.

Gaddis, Eugene R. *Magician of the Modern: Chick Austin and the Transformation of the Arts in America*. New York: Alfred A. Knopf, 2000.

Gammell, Sereno B. "Twain Mansion Drew Attention from Beginning." *Hartford Times*, November 1, 1935.

Geer's Hartford City Directory for the Year Commencing July, 1876. Hartford: Elihu Geer, 1876.

Haley, Jacquetta M. *Furnishings Plan: The Kitchen Wing, the Mark Twain House, Hartford, Connecticut*. Ridgefield, CT: Haley Research & Consulting, 2004.

———. *Furnishings Plan: The Mark Twain House, Hartford, Connecticut*. Ridgefield, CT: Haley Research & Consulting, 2004.

Howells, William Dean. *My Mark Twain*. Mineola, NY: Dover, 1997 (reprint of 1910 edition).

Jerome, Robert D., Barbara Snedecor, and Herbert A. Wisbey, eds. *Mark Twain in Elmira*. Elmira, NY: Elmira College, 2013.

Kaplan, Justin. *Mr. Clemens and Mark Twain: A Biography*. New York: Simon & Schuster, 1966.

Landau, Sarah Bradford. *Edward T. and William A. Potter: American Victorian Architects*. New York: Garland Publishing, 1979.

———. "Mark Twain's House in Connecticut." *Architectural Review* 169, no. 1009 (1981): 162–66.

Mac Donnell, Kevin. "George Griffin: Meeting Mark Twain's Butler Face to Face." *Mark Twain Journal* 62, no. 1 (2024): 10–58.

Mark Twain in Hartford. Hartford, CT: Mark Twain Memorial, 1958.

"Mark Twain's House." *Elmira* (NY) *Advertiser*, January 30, 1874.

Meltzer, Milton. *Mark Twain Himself*. New York: Wings Books, 1960.

Paine, Albert Bigelow. *Mark Twain: A Biography*, vols. 1–4. New York and London: Harper & Brothers, 1912.

Pfeffer, Miki. *A New Orleans Writer in Mark Twain's Court: Letters from Grace King's New England Sojourns*. Baton Rouge: Louisiana State University Press, 2019.

Rasmussen, R. Kent. *Mark Twain A to Z: The Essential Reference to His Life and Writings*. New York: Facts on File, 1995.

Salsbury, Edith Colgate. *Susy and Mark Twain: Family Dialogues*. New York: Harper & Row, 1965.

Schwinn, Walter K. "Mark Twain's Hartford House." Unpublished manuscript in The Mark Twain House & Museum Archive, 1986.

Snedecor, Barbara, ed. *Gravity: Selected Letters of Olivia Langdon Clemens*. Columbia: University of Missouri Press, 2023.

Thayer, Lee. *Murder Stalks the Circle*. New York: Dodd, Mead & Co., 1947.

Twain, Mark. *Collected Tales, Sketches, Speeches, & Essays, 1852–1890*. Edited by Louis J. Budd. New York: Library of America, 1992.

Twichell, Joseph H. "Mark Twain." *Harper's New Monthly Magazine*, May 1896.

Warner, Charles Dudley. *The Complete Writings of Charles Dudley Warner*, 15 vols. Edited by Thomas Lounsbury. Hartford, CT: American Publishing Co., 1904.

Willis, Resa. *Mark and Livy: The Love Story of Mark Twain and the Woman Who Almost Tamed Him*. New York: Atheneum, 1992.

About the Author

Steve Courtney is the author of *Joseph Hopkins Twichell: The Life and Times of Mark Twain's Closest Friend* (2008), winner of the Connecticut Book Award; *"The Loveliest Home That Ever Was": The Story of the Mark Twain House in Hartford* (2011; revision by Globe Pequot 2025); and *Mark Twain's Hartford* (2016), among other works. He is coeditor, with Peter Messent of the University of Nottingham and Harold K. Bush of St. Louis University, of *The Letters of Mark Twain and Joseph Hopkins Twichell* (2017, paperback edition 2020). He has been a journalist for forty years, much of that time at the *Hartford Courant*, and has served as both publicist and curatorial project coordinator at The Mark Twain House & Museum in Hartford, Connecticut.